LIBRARY PUBLISHING DIRECTORY
2016

EDITED BY SARAH K. LIPPINCOTT

Library
Publishing
Coalition

1230 PEACHTREE STREET, SUITE 1900
ATLANTA, GA 30309
WWW.LIBRARYPUBLISHING.ORG
919.533.9814
SARAH@EDUCOPIA.ORG

978-0-9899118-6-3 (PRINT)
978-0-9899118-7-0 (EPUB)
978-0-9899118-8-7 (EPDF)

CONTENTS

Introduction   vi
Library Publishing Coalition Committees   x
Reading an Entry   xii

LIBRARIES IN THE UNITED STATES AND CANADA

Boston College   2
Brigham Young University   4
Brock University   6
Cal Poly, San Luis Obispo   8
Carnegie Mellon University   10
Clemson University   12
Colby College   14
College at Brockport, State University of New York   16
College of William and Mary   18
Columbia University   20
Cornell University   22
Dartmouth College   24
DePaul University   26
Duke University   28
East Carolina University   30
Embry-Riddle Aeronautical University   32
Emory University   34
Florida International University   36
Florida State University   38
George Fox University   40
George Mason University   42
Georgetown University   44
Gettysburg College   46
Grand Valley State University   48
Gustavus Adolphus College   50
Illinois Wesleyan University   52
Indiana University   54
Indiana University Purdue University Indianapolis (IUPUI) 56
Iowa State University   58
James Madison University   60
Johns Hopkins University   62
Kansas State University   64
Linfield College   66
Loyola University Chicago   68
Macalester College   70
McGill University   73
McMaster University   75
Northeastern University   77
Northwestern University   79

Ohio State University	81
Oregon State University	83
Pacific University	86
Pennsylvania State University	88
Pepperdine University	91
Portland State University	93
Purdue University	95
Queen's University	98
Rutgers University	100
Seattle Pacific University	102
Simon Fraser University	104
Southern Illinois University Carbondale	106
St. Thomas University	108
SUNY Geneseo	109
SUNY Plattsburgh	111
Syracuse University	113
Temple University	116
Tulane University	118
Université Laval	120
University of Alberta	121
University of Arizona	123
University of British Columbia	125
University of California	127
University of Chicago	129
University of Florida	130
University of Guelph	132
University of Hawaii at Manoa	134
University of Illinois at Chicago	136
University of Illinois Urbana-Champaign	138
University of Iowa	140
University of Kansas	142
University of Kentucky	144
University of Maryland	147
University of Massachusetts Amherst	149
University of Massachusetts Medical School	152
University of Miami	154
University of Michigan	156
University of Minnesota	158
University of Nebraska-Lincoln	160
University of New Orleans	162
University of North Carolina at Chapel Hill	164
University of North Carolina at Charlotte	166
University of North Carolina at Greensboro	168
University of North Texas	170
University of Oklahoma	172
University of Oregon	174
University of Pittsburgh	176

University of Puget Sound   179
University of Richmond   181
University of San Diego   183
University of South Florida   184
University of Tennessee   186
University of Texas at Arlington   189
University of Virginia   191
University of Washington   193
University of Waterloo   195
University of Wisconsin–Milwaukee   197
Valparaiso University   199
Vanderbilt University   201
Villanova University   203
Virginia Commonwealth University   205
Virginia Tech   207
Wake Forest University   210
Washington University in St. Louis   212
Wayne State University   214
Western Washington University   216

LIBRARIES OUTSIDE NORTH AMERICA

Australian National University   219
Georg-August-Universität Göttingen   221
Monash University   223
Stockholm University   225
Swinburne University of Technology   227
University of Craiova, Romania   229
University of Huddersfield   231
University of Manchester   233
University of Technology, Sydney   235
UWE Bristol   237

Library Publishing Coalition Strategic Affiliates   238
Platforms, Tools, and Service Providers   239
Personnel Index   243

INTRODUCTION

Sarah K. Lippincott

We are very pleased to bring you this third edition of the *Library Publishing Directory*. This year, the *Directory* compiles the latest information on the publishing initiatives of 115 libraries from the United States, Canada, Australia, the United Kingdom, Sweden, and Romania.

As we assemble each edition of the *Directory*, we keep our numerous overlapping audiences in mind. We create the *Directory* as a resource for librarians, university administrators, scholars, and publishing and scholarly communications professionals. While the *Directory* has multiple distinct uses that we hope serve each of these groups, the most fundamental is to identify and forge connections among this growing community of peers. We hope that librarians, publishing professionals, and scholars alike will consult the *Directory* to learn more about and engage with these pathbreaking publishing programs. However, the significance and value of the *Directory* goes beyond this straightforward use. It demonstrates the depth, breadth, and sophistication of the field. The rich dataset aggregated within the *Directory* has been mined by the LPC and many others to gain important insights about the practices and principles of library publishing. It is our hope that this *Directory* inspires libraries to launch or expand publishing services, and that it encourages the formation of additional research partnerships across multiple sectors.

While the specifics of each edition differ, the general trends, themes, and principles have remained compellingly consistent. The entries in this *Directory* continue to demonstrate librarians' engagement with new modes of scholarship, such as the many multimedia, interdisciplinary, and nontraditional publications referenced herein. The entries also underscore libraries' commitments to campus teaching and learning, as illustrated by the many libraries herein that are currently involved in the publication of student research journals, open educational resources, textbooks, and other student-oriented outputs. They also reveal a dedication to developing sustainable publishing models that ensure that scholars, students, and the general public gain access to high-quality scholarship. The variety of partnerships (with university presses, scholarly societies, and others) that libraries have undertaken, for example, often demonstrate value and sustainability at their core.

The *Library Publishing Directory* is produced by the Library Publishing Coalition (LPC), a growing, international community of academic and research libraries that is committed to advancing the field of library publishing. The LPC's Directory Committee maintains the *Directory* and ensures that all print and digital versions are useful, current, and accurate. Joshua Neds-Fox (Wayne State University) chaired this year's committee, and Katherine Purple (Purdue University) coordinated production of the *Directory.* Committee members Char Simser (Kansas State University) and Terry Owen (University of Maryland), and LPC Board Liaison Korey Jackson (Oregon State University), contributed significant time and effort, from improving our data collection process to editing early drafts of the entries.

We collected updates and new entries for the *Directory* during July and August 2015. Libraries that appeared in last year's edition were contacted directly, and e-mails soliciting new entries were distributed to major library e-mail lists and social media channels in July 2015. As in previous years, we primarily targeted libraries in the United States and Canada, but also received numerous submissions from around the world, including Australia, the United Kingdom, South Africa, Sweden, and Germany.

LIBRARY PUBLISHING LANDSCAPE

The 2016 data reinforce many of the trends we observed last year: commitment to partnerships, lean workforces, diverse service offerings, and an emphasis on open access models. Below, we present a few highlights based on a preliminary analysis of the data.

The vast majority of respondents partner with campus departments or programs (93%) and individual faculty (91%). Sixty-nine percent also work with graduate students, and 57% partner with undergraduates. Thirty of the 115 libraries profiled in this publication list at least one university press partner, typically the press on their campus, but also frequently presses at other institutions. Other notable partners include scholarly societies, library consortia and networks, non-profit organizations, and museums.

The data confirm that most libraries focus on local publications (i.e., content produced by or affiliated with their students, faculty, research centers, or departments). Libraries published a total of 404 faculty-driven, campus-based journal titles during the period covered by the questionnaire (2014–2015). On average, each library publishes approximately five faculty-driven, campus-based journals. Libraries also published 224 campus-based, student-driven journal titles in 2014–2015. This was the only category of journal that saw growth since last year, even though the total number of respondents for this year was slightly lower. Despite the emphasis on local content, libraries do not deal exclusively with campus-based publications. The libraries listed herein published 189 journal titles under contract/MOU for external groups (such as faculty from other institutions, scholarly societies, or research institutes). They also publish an average of five journals under contract, though there are a few outliers that have portfolios of dozens of journals.

Libraries reported a total of 773 monographs published in 2014–2015. Three libraries—the California Digital Library, Cornell University, and Indiana University—account for 478 of those titles. Other popular publications include technical/research reports, faculty and/or student conference papers and proceedings, ETDs, and undergraduate capstones/honors theses.

Libraries overwhelmingly report that their services are partially or fully funded by the library's operating budget, a statistic that affirms the positioning of publishing as a library service. Ninety-four percent of responding libraries receive part (44%) or all (56%) of their funding from the library's operating budget. None of the libraries featured in the *Directory* receives all (or even a majority) of its funding through revenue streams such as sales and licensing. Eleven libraries report they generate some revenue from sales, 2 from licensing, and 6 from charge-backs to content creators. Other sources of funding include the library materials budget, non-library campus funds, and grants.

Lean staffing continues to characterize library publishing initiatives. Libraries report a range of .1 to 14.5 full-time equivalent (FTE) in professional staff directly supporting publishing activities. The average FTE for professional staff reported this year was 2.4 (an increase over last year's reported average of 1.8 FTE). Libraries also report an average of 1 FTE in paraprofessional staff, .8 FTE in graduate student support, and 1 FTE in undergraduate student support. Approximately half of respondents benefit from paraprofessional staff support for their publishing programs. Nineteen percent have graduate student employees and 30 percent employ undergraduate student workers.

Slightly over half of respondents report that their publishing activities are centralized in one library unit, while the remainder report that services are spread across various units in the library or around campus. As we noted in last year's *Directory*, library publishing activities are housed within a range of library units, including Digital Scholarship, Digital Initiatives, Scholarly Communications, and Collections; and are led by librarians at all levels, from early-career librarians to associate deans, with titles such as Scholarly Communication Librarian, Head of Digital Scholarship or Digital Scholarship Librarian, Director of Digital Publishing, and Digital Initiatives Librarian. Nineteen of the librarians listed as the lead contact for their publishing program have the word "Publishing" in their title.

In addition to hosting, supporting, and/or building a publishing platform, libraries report offering a suite of auxiliary services that support production, dissemination, and preservation. Many of the most popular additional services build upon traditional library skills, such as user education and outreach, information management, and digital technologies. The majority of respondents reported that they provide copyright advisory (93%), training (91%), metadata services (88%), digitization (82%), hosting of supplemental content (77%), analytics (73%), cataloging (68%), outreach (61%), and ISSN assignment (58%). Most libraries also report that they provide some form of digital preservation for their content, though many do not offer preservation beyond in-house backups of content. Notably, many of the services less commonly provided by libraries are integral parts of the traditional publishing enterprise, including core production and management services. Fewer than 25% of respondents provide notification of abstracting and indexing sources (28%), copy-editing (24%), typesetting (22%), print-on-demand (21%), image services (21%), business model development (15%), creation of indexes (11%), and budget preparation (9%) in 2014–2015.

Libraries rely on a variety of open source, commercial, and locally built publishing technologies. Thirty-seven percent of respondents use only one publishing platform or software, while the great majority use multiple platforms and other tools. Popular publishing platforms include OJS (43%) and bepress (42%), followed by DSpace (31%), WordPress (25%), locally developed software (23%), CONTENTdm (19%), Fedora (16%), and OCS, OMP, EPrints, Islandora, Hydra, Scalar, Drupal, Tizra, Omeka, Biblioboard, and DPubS (each with less than 10% usage).

As we continue to update the *Directory* in the coming years, we hope to provide the community with an increasingly rich dataset that enables new insights and improves practices in the field. We thank all the libraries who participated in this year's edition for contributing their time and information to this endeavor.

LIBRARY PUBLISHING COALITION COMMITTEES

The Board and Committee Members listed below have donated their time and expertise to advancing the Library Publishing Coalition's mission and furthering the field of library publishing.

BOARD OFFICERS
Brad Eden, Valparaiso University (President)
Kevin Hawkins, University of North Texas (Immediate-Past President)
Catherine Mitchell, California Digital Library (President-Elect)
Scott Walter, DePaul University (Treasurer)

BOARD MEMBERS
Sarah Beaubien, Grand Valley State University
Isaac Gilman, Pacific University
Korey Jackson, Oregon State University
Marcia Stockham, Kansas State University
Sarah Melton, Emory University
Sarah Lippincott, Library Publishing Coalition (ex officio)

DIRECTORY COMMITTEE
Joshua Neds-Fox, Wayne State (chair)
Char Simser, Kansas State University
Terry Owen, University of Maryland
Katherine Purple, Purdue University

PROGRAM COMMITTEE
Sarah Beaubien, Grand Valley State University (chair)
William Kane, Wake Forest University
David Scherer, Carnegie Mellon University
Catherine Mitchell, California Digital Library
Scott Walter, DePaul University
Somaly Kim Wu, UNC-Charlotte
Vanessa Gabler, University of Pittsburgh
Melanie Schlosser, Ohio State University

RESEARCH COMMITTEE
Harrison Inefuku, Iowa State University
Allegra Swift, Claremont Colleges
Kelly Riddle, University of San Diego
Gail McMillan, Virginia Tech
Isaac Gilman, Pacific University

FINANCE COMMITTEE

Scott Walter, DePaul University (treasurer)
Sarah Melton, Emory University
Jeff Rubin, Tulane University
Mary Beth Thomson, University of Kentucky
Marcia Stockham, Kansas State University
Jason Coleman, University of Michigan
Kevin Hawkins, University of North Texas

MEMBERSHIP COMMITTEE

Charles Watkinson, University of Michigan
Korey Jackson, Oregon State University
Wendy Robertson, University of Iowa
Andrew Rouner, Washington University

PROFESSIONAL DEVELOPMENT COMMITTEE

Meredith Kahn, University of Michigan
Adrian Ho, University of Kentucky
Yu-Hung Lin, Rutgers University
Kate McCready, University of Minnesota
Hillary Corbett, Northeastern University
Jonathan Bull, Valparaiso University

READING AN ENTRY: SOME "HEALTH WARNINGS"

Collecting and synthesizing the information provided by over 100 libraries in an evolving and experimental subfield like library-based publishing presents numerous challenges. Even in this third edition, we are refining our approach to data collection and presentation. We are pleased to present what we believe is the most accurate and complete *Directory* to date; but we ask that you continue to bear with minor inconsistencies that appear across entries.

Each of the entries in the *Directory* undergoes minor editing for style and consistency, but we largely leave it up to libraries to present their publishing programs as they see fit. As we reminded readers last year, labeling and categorizing the diverse set of "library publishing" activities is no easy feat; nor is setting boundaries around funding streams, staffing, and services that bear specifically on library publishing activities.

Respondents were instructed to base their answers on the last twelve months of their library activity, a period covering roughly July 2014 to July 2015. In some cases, questions in the questionnaire on which the entries are based still need to be clarified in order to ensure that we collect consistent data. For instance, we continue to note inconsistencies in the way that institutions report the numbers of publications they produce, with some reporting numbers of publications that were made available *for the first time* within the last twelve months and others reporting cumulative numbers of publications as of the date they completed the survey.

While we aim to present a full picture of the field, the *Directory* does not claim to be comprehensive. The questionnaire we use to collect data for the *Directory* was distributed to major library e-mail lists and forums in the United States and Canada and directly to representatives of all the libraries featured in last year's edition. As in previous years, the majority of entries come from these regions, though there are a number of excellent programs from around the world represented herein.

Finally, readers will notice the presence of "seals" next to the title of some entries. These acknowledge the support of our Library Publishing Coalition Members and our Founding Institutions, who each provided $5,000 a year for two-years to seed fund the organization. To recognize their exceptional contributions, we include profiles of specific publications that Founding Institutions have nominated. These also give a practical sense of the wide range of types of publications produced.

We look forward to continuing to produce and improve the *Directory* with the input and participation of this vibrant community.

FOUNDER

LIBRARIES IN THE
UNITED STATES AND CANADA

BOSTON COLLEGE
Boston College University Libraries

Primary Unit: Scholarly Communications and Research

Primary Contact: Jane Morris
Head Librarian, Scholarly Communications and Research
617-552-4481
jane.morris@bc.edu

PROGRAM OVERVIEW
Mission statement: The Boston College University Libraries' publishing program showcases and preserves Boston College's scholarly output in digital form and makes it freely accessible globally. The institutional repository, eScholarship@ BC, is a publishing platform for student theses and juried work and for faculty scholarship. Open access journals provide faculty, student groups, and academic centers with a platform and services for production and publication of high-quality scholarship. The Libraries' publishing program supports the social justice mission of the University and promotes the goals of the University Libraries by providing access to scholarly resources wherever they are needed.

Year publishing activities began: 2006

Organization: services are distributed across library units/departments

Total FTE in support of publishing activities: professional staff (3.5)

Funding sources (%): library operating budget (100)

PUBLISHING ACTIVITIES
Library publications in 2015: campus-based faculty-driven journals (1); campus-based student-driven journals (4); journals produced under contract/MOU for external groups (4); monographs (1); faculty conference papers and proceedings (2); newsletters (1); ETDs (156); undergraduate capstones/honors theses (30)

Media formats: text; images; video; data

Disciplinary specialties: theology; education

Top publications: *Information Technology and Libraries* (journal); *Studies in Christian-Jewish Relations* (journal); *Proceedings of the Catholic Theological Society of America* (conference proceedings); *Levantine Review* (journal)

Percentage of journals that are peer reviewed: 25

Internal partners: campus departments or programs; individual faculty; graduate students; undergraduate students

External partners: Catholic Theological Society of America; ALA Library and Information Technology Association; Council of Centers on Christian-Jewish Relations; Seminar on Jesuit Spirituality

Publishing platform(s): OJS; Islandora

Digital preservation strategy: HathiTrust; LOCKSS; MetaArchive

Additional services: marketing; outreach; training; analytics; cataloging; metadata; ISSN registry; DOI assignment/allocation of identifiers; open URL support; dataset management; contract/license preparation; author copyright advisory; digitization; audio/video streaming

ADDITIONAL INFORMATION

Plans for expansion/future directions: We plan to increase outreach efforts to capture more research data and scholarly publications. We are considering an additional data repository option. We are working to provide more services to those who publish open access journals with our program.

BRIGHAM YOUNG UNIVERSITY
Harold B. Lee Library

Library Publishing Coalition — MEMBER INSTITUTION

FOUNDER

Primary Unit: Scholarly Communication Unit
scholarsarchive@byu.edu

Primary Contact: Mandy Oscarson
Scholarly Communication Services Manager
801-422-7663
mandy_oscarson@byu.edu

Website: scholarsarchive.byu.edu

PROGRAM OVERVIEW

Mission statement: Harold B. Lee Library's primary publishing resources include an institutional repository and digital publishing services for faculty- and student-edited journals. Combined, these resources are called ScholarsArchive. ScholarsArchive is designed to make original scholarly and creative work—such as research, publications, journals, and data—freely and persistently available. The library's publishing efforts are targeted at supporting broader academic and public discovery and use of university scholarship. ScholarsArchive may also house items of historic interest to the university. The library supports content partners with software support, digitizing, metadata creation, journal management, and free hosting services.

Year publishing activities began: 2001

Organization: centralized library publishing unit/department

Total FTE in support of publishing activities: library staff (1.25); undergraduate students (0.5)

Funding sources (%): library operating budget (98); charge backs (2)

PUBLISHING ACTIVITIES

Library publications in 2015: campus-based faculty-driven journals (8); campus-based student-driven journals (4); monographs (8); faculty conference papers and proceedings (135); student conference papers and proceedings (22); ETDs (1,095)

Media formats: text; images

Disciplinary specialties: religion; natural history of the American West; children's literature

Top publications: *Journal of East Asian Libraries* (journal); *BYU Studies* (journal); *Comparative Civilizations Review* (journal); *Pacific Studies* (journal); *TESL Reporter* (journal)

Percentage of journals that are peer reviewed: 90

Internal partners: campus departments or programs; individual faculty; graduate students; undergraduate students

External partners: International Society for the Comparative Study of Civilizations (ISCSC); Association of Mormon Counselors and Psychotherapists (AMCAP); Council on East Asian Libraries (CEAL)

Publishing platform(s): bepress (Digital Commons); CONTENTdm; OJS/OCS/OMP

Digital preservation strategy: Rosetta

Additional services: analytics; cataloging; metadata; peer review management; digitization; hosting of supplemental content

ADDITIONAL INFORMATION
Plans for expansion/future directions: Areas of future exploration and possible expansion include monograph publishing, print-on-demand, DOI support, hosting streaming media, hosting conferences, and data management.

HIGHLIGHTED PUBLICATION

The *Western North American Naturalist* (formerly *Great Basin Naturalist*) has published peer-reviewed experimental and descriptive research pertaining to the biological natural history of western North America for more than 70 years.

ojs.lib.byu.edu/spc/index.php/wnan

BROCK UNIVERSITY
James A. Gibson Library

Primary Unit: Library
eyates@brocku.ca

Primary Contact: Elizabeth Yates
Liaison/Scholarly Communication Librarian
905-688-5550 x4469
eyates@brocku.ca

Website: www.brocku.ca/library/about-us-lib/openaccess

PROGRAM OVERVIEW
Mission statement: The library's publishing initiatives provide technology, expertise, and promotional support for researchers, students, and staff at Brock University seeking to make their research universally accessible via open access. The library's current publishing activities include: publishing several scholarly OA journals in partnership with Scholars Portal and the Ontario Council of University Libraries using Open Journal Systems software and hosting and disseminating Brock scholarship through our Digital Repository, which collects graduate theses, major research projects, and subject- or department-based research collections.

Year publishing activities began: 2010

Organization: services are distributed across library units/departments

Total FTE in support of publishing activities: professional staff (1)

Funding sources (%): library materials budget (10); library operating budget (90)

PUBLISHING ACTIVITIES
Media formats: text; images

Disciplinary specialties: education; humanities; social justice

Percentage of journals that are peer reviewed: 100

Internal partners: campus departments or programs; individual faculty; graduate students

External partners: Scholars Portal/Ontario Council of University Libraries

Publishing platform(s): DSpace; OJS

Digital preservation strategy: Scholars Portal

Additional services: copy-editing; training; analytics; notification of A&I sources; ISSN registry; digitization

ADDITIONAL INFORMATION
Plans for expansion/future directions: We plan to expand our institutional repository to encourage wider deposit by Brock University researchers. We will also be adding at least one more scholarly open access journal in 2014–2015.

CAL POLY, SAN LUIS OBISPO
Robert E. Kennedy Library

Primary Unit: Academic Services

Primary Contact: Dana Ospina
Open Education Library Fellow
805-756-7581
dospina@calpoly.edu

PROGRAM OVERVIEW
Mission statement: The Robert E. Kennedy Library provides digital services to assist the campus community with the creation, publication, sharing, and preservation of research, scholarship, and campus history.

Year publishing activities began: 2008

Organization: services are distributed across library units/departments

Total FTE in support of publishing activities: professional staff (1); paraprofessional staff (1); undergraduate students (1)

Funding sources (%): library operating budget (100)

PUBLISHING ACTIVITIES
Library publications in 2015: campus-based faculty-driven journals (2); campus-based student-driven journals (1); monographs (1); technical/research reports (55); faculty conference papers and proceedings (325); student conference papers and proceedings (65); newsletters (7); ETDs (134); digital learning objects

Media formats: text; images; video; data; concept maps, modeling, maps, or other visualizations; multimedia/interactive content

Disciplinary specialties: science; history; philosophy; literature; communications

Top publications: master's theses; senior projects; *Forum* (journal); *Between the Species* (journal); *Focus* (journal)

Percentage of journals that are peer reviewed: 100

Internal partners: campus departments or programs; individual faculty; graduate students; undergraduate students

Publishing platform(s): bepress (Digital Commons)

Digital preservation strategy: Archive-It; discoverygarden; LOCKSS; MetaArchive

Additional services: outreach; training; DOI assignment/allocation of identifiers; peer review management; author copyright advisory; other author advisory; digitization; hosting of supplemental content

ADDITIONAL INFORMATION
Plans for expansion/future directions: The library plans to expand our program to include multi-format publications as well as curation and publishing of local image collections.

CARNEGIE MELLON UNIVERSITY
Carnegie Mellon University Libraries

Primary Unit: Scholarly Publishing, Archives, and Data Services

Primary Contact: Denise Troll Covey
Scholarly Communications Librarian
412-268-8599
troll@andrew.cmu.edu

PROGRAM OVERVIEW
Mission statement: Carnegie Mellon University Libraries' publishing program aims to promote open access to scholarly resources by publishing gray literature, including theses, dissertations, and technical reports in our open access repository, Research Showcase @ CMU.

Year publishing activities began: 2010

Organization: services are distributed across library units/departments

Total FTE in support of publishing activities: professional staff (1); paraprofessional staff (0.5)

Funding sources (%): library operating budget (100)

PUBLISHING ACTIVITIES
Library publications in 2015: campus-based faculty-driven journals (1); technical/research reports (75); ETDs (200); undergraduate capstones/honors theses (32)

Media formats: text

Disciplinary specialties: social and behavioral sciences; engineering; physical and life sciences; arts and humanities; security

Top publications: computer science (repository series); Dietrich College honors theses (repository series); dissertations (repository series); *Journal of Privacy and Confidentiality* (journal); robotics (repository series)

Percentage of journals that are peer reviewed: 100

Internal partners: campus departments or programs; individual faculty; graduate students; undergraduate students

Publishing platform(s): bepress (Digital Commons)

Digital preservation strategy: LOCKSS; MetaArchive

Additional services: marketing; outreach; training; analytics; cataloging; metadata; author copyright advisory; other author advisory; digitization hosting of supplemental content; audio/video streaming

ADDITIONAL INFORMATION
Plans for expansion/future directions: We plan to migrate our IR from bepress Digital Commons to Fedora Hydra in 2016.

CLEMSON UNIVERSITY
R.M. Cooper Library

Primary Unit: Library Technology
vinsonc@clemson.edu

Primary Contact: Andrew Wesolek
Head of Digital Scholarship
864-656-0317
awesole@clemson.edu

Website: tigerprints.clemson.edu

PROGRAM OVERVIEW
Mission statement: R.M. Cooper Library supports the production and dissemination of knowledge at Clemson University through the entirety of the scholarly communication lifecycle. As part of this effort, we offer the infrastructure and expertise to support the publishing of scholarly significant works that may not have another avenue for publication. These include theses and dissertations, student produced research posters, conference proceedings, two open access journals, open educational resources, and more.

Year publishing activities began: 2006

Total FTE in support of publishing activities: professional staff (1); paraprofessional staff (2); undergraduates (1)

Funding sources (%): library operating budget (100)

PUBLISHING ACTIVITIES
Library publications in 2015: campus-based faculty-driven journals (1); faculty conference papers and proceedings (50); newsletters (1); ETDs (300); student research posters (490)

Media formats: text; images; video

Disciplinary specialties: South Carolina water resources

Top publications: NASIG Newsletter; *South Carolina Water Resources Conference* (conference proceedings); *Journal of South Carolina Water Resources* (journal)

Percentage of journals that are peer reviewed: 50

Internal partners: individual faculty

External partners: NASIG

Publishing platform(s): bepress (Digital Commons)

Digital preservation strategy: MetaArchive

Additional services: training; analytics; metadata; dataset management; author copyright advisory

ADDITIONAL INFORMATION
Plans for expansion/future directions: We are in the very early stages of a partnership with Clemson Online to promote the creation and adoption of Open Educational Resources. We expect that the Libraries will serve as publisher of newly created OER.

COLBY COLLEGE
Colby College Libraries

FOUNDER

Primary Unit: Digital & Special Collections

Primary Contact: Martin Kelly
Assistant Director for Digital Collections
207-859-5162
martin.kelly@colby.edu

Website: www.colby.edu/specialcollections

PROGRAM OVERVIEW

Mission statement: The publishing mission of Colby College Libraries Digital and Special Collections is to showcase the scholarly and creative work of Colby's faculty and students, make the college's unique collections more broadly available, and contribute to open intellectual discourse.

Organization: centralized library publishing unit/department

Total FTE in support of publishing activities: professional staff (1); paraprofessional staff (1); undergraduate students (1.5)

Funding sources (%): library operating budget (100)

PUBLISHING ACTIVITIES

Library publications in 2015: campus-based faculty-driven journals (2); campus-based student-driven journals (1); monographs (2); technical/research reports (125); student conference papers and proceedings (1); newsletters (72); undergraduate capstones/honors theses (88); individual faculty SelectedWorks sites; course-related projects (12); college magazine issues (374); faculty articles (24)

Media formats: text; images; audio; video; data; concept maps, modeling, maps, or other visualizations

Disciplinary specialties: environmental studies; humanities; economics; Jewish studies; women, gender, and sexuality studies

Top publications: *Colby Quarterly* (journal); Honors Theses (repository series); Senior Scholar Papers (repository series); *Colby Magazine* (periodical); Undergraduate Research Symposium/Colby Liberal Arts Symposium (CLAS) (conference proceedings)

Percentage of journals that are peer reviewed: 66.6

Internal partners: campus departments or programs; individual faculty; undergraduate students

Publishing platform(s): bepress (Digital Commons); WordPress

Digital preservation strategy: digital preservation services under discussion

Additional services: graphic design (print or web); outreach; training; analytics; cataloging; metadata; open URL support; peer review management; author copyright advisory; digitization; image services; hosting of supplemental content; audio/video streaming

ADDITIONAL INFORMATION

Plans for expansion/future directions: Greater focus on special collections and institutional archives. Support for faculty and undergraduate datasets. Promotion of publishing support for faculty-edited undergraduate research journals.

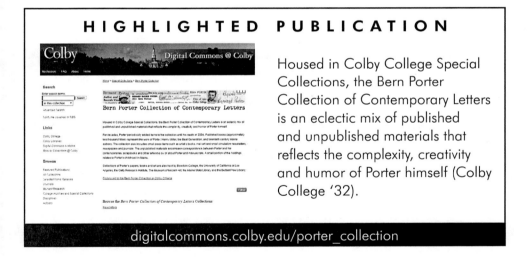

HIGHLIGHTED PUBLICATION

Housed in Colby College Special Collections, the Bern Porter Collection of Contemporary Letters is an eclectic mix of published and unpublished materials that reflects the complexity, creativity and humor of Porter himself (Colby College '32).

digitalcommons.colby.edu/porter_collection

COLLEGE AT BROCKPORT, STATE UNIVERSITY OF NEW YORK
Drake Memorial Library

Primary Unit: Library Technology
digitalcommons@brockport.edu

Primary Contact: Kim Myers
Digital Repository Specialist
585-395-2742
kmyers@brockport.edu

Website: digitalcommons.brockport.edu

PROGRAM OVERVIEW

Mission statement: To provide open access to the scholarly and creative works created by the community of the College at Brockport.

Year publishing activities began: 2012

Organization: centralized library publishing unit/department

Total FTE in support of publishing activities: professional staff (1.25)

Funding sources (%): library materials budget (100)

PUBLISHING ACTIVITIES

Library publications in 2015: campus-based faculty-driven journals (2); campus-based student-driven journals (2); monographs (1); technical/research reports (150); faculty conference papers and proceedings (23); student conference papers and proceedings (300); newsletters (7); databases (1); ETDs (765); undergraduate capstones/honors theses (35)

Media formats: text; images; audio; video; data

Disciplinary specialties: education; counselor education; philosophy; English; kinesiology and sports

Top publications: counselor education master's theses; education master's theses; *Philosophic Exchange* (journal); CMST Institute lesson plans; English master's theses

Percentage of journals that are peer reviewed: 50

16

Internal partners: campus departments or programs; individual faculty; graduate students; undergraduate students

Publishing platform(s): bepress (Digital Commons)

Digital preservation strategy: LOCKSS

Additional services: copy-editing; marketing; outreach; training; analytics; cataloging; metadata; ISSN registry; dataset management; author copyright advisory; digitization hosting of supplemental content

ADDITIONAL INFORMATION
Plans for expansion/future directions: Expand the ETD program, develop and support journals, and look into publishing original manuscripts from faculty and emeriti.

COLLEGE OF WILLIAM AND MARY
William & Mary Libraries

Primary Unit: Technology & Content Services
wmpublish@wm.edu

Primary Contact: Deborah Cornell
Head of Digital Services
757-221-3098
dacornell@wm.edu

PROGRAM OVERVIEW
Mission statement: W&M Publish is a service of the W&M Libraries that provides open access to the active research and scholarship produced by our faculty, staff, and students. The purpose of W&M Publish is to promote information discovery, collaboration, and to publicize the scholarly output of the College of William and Mary.

Year publishing activities began: 2014

Organization: centralized library publishing unit/department

Total FTE in support of publishing activities: professional staff (2)

Funding sources (%): library operating budget (100)

PUBLISHING ACTIVITIES
Library publications in 2015: campus-based student-driven journals (2); journals produced under contract/MOU for external groups (1); ETDs (150); undergraduate capstones/honors theses (150)

Media formats: text; images

Disciplinary specialties: American history; undergraduate research

Top publications: *Colonial Academic Alliance Undergraduate Research Journal* (journal); *James Blair Historical Review* (journal)

Percentage of journals that are peer reviewed: 33

Internal partners: campus departments or programs

Publishing platform(s): bepress (Digital Commons)

Digital preservation strategy: LOCKSS

Additional services: graphic design (print or web); training; author copyright advisory

ADDITIONAL INFORMATION
Plans for expansion/future directions: Our library is hiring the position of Digital Scholarship Librarian to lead and develop our OA and Scholarly Publishing program.

COLUMBIA UNIVERSITY
Columbia University Libraries

Primary Unit: Center for Digital Research and Scholarship
info@cdrs.columbia.edu

Primary Contact: Mark Newton
Interim Director and Production Manager
212-851-7337
mnewton@columbia.edu

Website: cdrs.columbia.edu

Social media: facebook.com/pages/Center-for-Digital-Research-and-Scholarship
-Columbia-University/63932011889; @ColumbiaCDRS; @ResearchAtCU;
@ScholarlyComm; @DataAtCU; instagram.com/columbiacdrs

PROGRAM OVERVIEW
Mission statement: The Center for Digital Research and Scholarship (CDRS)
serves the digital research and scholarly communications needs of the faculty,
students, and staff of Columbia University and its affiliates. Our mission is to
increase the utility and impact of research produced at Columbia by creating,
adapting, implementing, supporting, and sustaining innovative digital tools and
publishing platforms for content delivery, discovery, analysis, data curation, and
preservation. In pursuit of that mission, we also engage in extensive outreach,
education, and advocacy to ensure that the scholarly work produced at Columbia
University has a global reach and accelerates the pace of research across
disciplines.

Year publishing activities began: 1997 (Columbia University Libraries); 2007
(CDRS)

Organization: centralized library publishing unit/department

Total FTE in support of publishing activities: professional staff (14.5); graduate
students (0.5); undergraduate students (1.25)

PUBLISHING ACTIVITIES
Library publications in 2015: campus-based faculty-driven journals (3); campus-
based student-driven journals (17); technical/research reports (44); faculty
conference papers and proceedings (20); ETDs (207); undergraduate capstones/
honors theses (20)

Media formats: text; images; audio; video; data; software in repository

Disciplinary specialties: law; (digital) humanities; interdisciplinary studies

Top publications: Academic Commons (digital research repository); *Digital Dante* (scholarly website); *Tremor and Other Hyperkinetic Movements* (journal); *Women Film Pioneers Project* (database)

Percentage of journals that are peer reviewed: 90

Internal partners: campus departments or programs; individual faculty; graduate students; undergraduate students

External partners: Modern Language Association

University press partners: Columbia University Press; Fordham University Press

Publishing platform(s): Fedora; OJS; WordPress; locally developed software

Digital preservation strategy: Amazon S3; AP Trust; Archive-It; DuraCloud; DPN; in-house; digital preservation services under discussion; local databases are backed up and replicated locally; preservation content is also replicated to NYSRnet

Additional services: graphic design (print or web); print-on-demand; typesetting; copy-editing; marketing; outreach; training; analytics; cataloging; metadata; ISBN registry; DOI assignment/allocation of identifiers; dataset management; business model development; contract/license preparation; author copyright advisory; other author advisory; digitization; hosting of supplemental content; audio/video streaming; preservation; repository deposit to PMC; SEO; application development; content and platform migration; workshops and consultation; social media and journal publishing best practices workshops; scholarly communication and open access outreach and programming

ADDITIONAL INFORMATION

Additional information: Journal partners use external (non-CDRS) services and platforms to manage subscriptions, subscription revenues, and access to subscription-only content.

Plans for expansion/future directions: Future plans include expansion of data publication services within Academic Commons and continued integration of platforms between the journals and the repository. CDRS seeks to expand its journals program with the addition of new partners and publications, through enhanced marketing and outreach efforts, and through attention to underlying nontechnical infrastructure such as its publishing agreements.

CORNELL UNIVERSITY
Cornell University Library

Primary Unit: Digital Scholarship and Preservation Services

Primary Contact: David Ruddy
Director, Scholarly Communications Services
607-255-6803
dwr4@cornell.edu

PROGRAM OVERVIEW
Mission statement: Separate operations have their own mission statements (Project Euclid, arXiv, eCommons, Signale, CIP). In general, we wish to promote sustainable models of scholarly communications with an emphasis on access, affordability, and scale.

Year publishing activities began: 2000

Organization: services are distributed across library units/departments

Total FTE in support of publishing activities: professional staff (7.25); undergraduates (.4)

Funding sources (%): library operating budget (20); sales revenue (40); other (40)

PUBLISHING ACTIVITIES
Library publications in 2015: campus-based faculty-driven journals (3); campus-based student-driven journals (1); journals produced under contract/MOU for external groups (70); monographs (185); textbooks (1); technical/research reports (90,000); faculty conference papers and proceedings (2); ETDs (700); undergraduate capstones/honors theses (50)

Media formats: text; audio; video; data

Disciplinary specialties: mathematics; physics; statistics; computer science; modern German cultural history

Top publications: arXiv.org (repository); Project Euclid (journal platform); *Signale* (monograph series)

Percentage of journals that are peer reviewed: 100

Internal partners: campus departments or programs; individual faculty; graduate students; undergraduate students

External partners: scholarly societies; scholars worldwide

University press partners: Duke University Press

Publishing platform(s): DPubS; DSpace; locally developed software

Digital preservation strategy: in-house

Additional services: graphic design (print or web); print-on-demand; analytics; metadata; DOI assignment/allocation of identifiers; open URL support; business model development; budget preparation; digitization; hosting of supplemental content; audio/video streaming

DARTMOUTH COLLEGE
Dartmouth College Library

Library Publishing Coalition — MEMBER INSTITUTION

FOUNDER

Primary Unit: Digital Library Program

Primary Contact: Barbara DeFelice
Program Director for Scholarly Communication, Copyright and Publishing
603-646-3565
barbara.defelice@dartmouth.edu

Website: www.dartmouth.edu/~library/digital/publishing/index.html

PROGRAM OVERVIEW
Mission statement: The Dartmouth Library's Digital Publishing Program focuses on providing open access, online publishing of scholarly publications that are created by Dartmouth faculty or students, or are published by Dartmouth. Selected digital exhibits and faculty-generated web-based collections of scholarly content are also in scope. All content published in this program is available online without charge.

Year publishing activities began: 2002

Organization: services are distributed across library units/departments

Total FTE in support of publishing activities: library staff (3.75)

Funding sources (%): library operating budget (10); endowment income (10); other (80)

PUBLISHING ACTIVITIES
Media formats: text; images; audio; video; data; concept maps/modeling maps/ visualizations; multimedia/interactive content

Disciplinary specialties: environment; linguistics; electronic or "new" media; Native American history; history of Arctic exploration

Top publications: *Elementa* (journal); *Linguistic Discovery* (journal); *Journal of E-Media Studies* (journal); Occom Circle Project (digital collection); *Artistry of the Homeric Simile* (monograph); *Black London: Life Before Emancipation* (monograph)

Percentage of journals that are peer reviewed: 100

Internal partners: campus departments and programs; individual faculty; student journal editors

External partners: BioOne

University press partners: University Press of New England

Publishing platform(s): CONTENTdm; locally developed software

Digital preservation strategy: DPN; HathiTrust; LOCKSS; Portico; in-house; digital preservation services under discussion

Additional services: marketing; outreach; training; analytics; cataloging; metadata; ISSN registry; DOI assignment/allocation of identifiers; open URL support; peer review management; business model development; budget preparation; other author advisory; digitization; audio/video streaming; XML consultation in JATS and TEI

ADDITIONAL INFORMATION
Additional information: The partnership with the publisher BioOne is enabling us to increase our our technological capacity for journal publishing. BioOne is a significant contributor to the staffing for Elementa. The partnership with the University Press of New England is enabling us to increase knowledge and capacity for monograph publishing.

Plans for expansion/future directions: Publishing more monographs in conjunction with the University Press of New England, further developing technical capacity for journals, increasing the number of digital editions, building out our services for student journals.

HIGHLIGHTED PUBLICATION

A mission-driven, nonprofit collaborative, *Elementa: Science of the Anthropocene* is a trans-disciplinary, open-access journal committed to the facilitation of collaborative, peer-reviewed research. It is uniquely structured into six distinct knowledge domains.

home.elementascience.org

DEPAUL UNIVERSITY
DePaul University Library

Primary Unit: Digital Services

Primary Contact: M. Ryan Hess
Digital Services Coordinator
773-325-7829
mhess8@depaul.edu

Website: via.library.depaul.edu

PROGRAM OVERVIEW

Mission statement: DePaul University Library's institutional repository, Via Sapientiae, supports DePaul's goal of academic enhancement by collecting, organizing, and providing open access to scholarly works in online curriculum vitae, book, journal, conference proceeding, and theses and dissertation form, produced by the University's faculty, staff, centers and institutes, and students.

Year publishing activities began: 2007

Organization: services are distributed across campus

Total FTE in support of publishing activities: professional staff (2); paraprofessional staff (1); graduate students (1)

PUBLISHING ACTIVITIES

Library publications in 2015: campus-based student-driven journals (2); monographs (2); technical/research reports (2); ETDs (60); student projects; student maps; student translations of historical documents

Media formats: text; images; audio; concept maps, modeling, maps, or other visualizations

Disciplinary specialties: Vincentian studies; business; law; French literature; science

Top publications: Theses and Dissertations (repository series); *Vincentian Heritage Journal* (journal); *Vincentiana* (journal); *DePaul Discoveries* (journal); *Journal of Religion and Business Ethics* (journal)

Percentage of journals that are peer reviewed: 100

Internal partners: campus departments or programs; individual faculty

External partners: Congregation of the Mission

Publishing platform(s): bepress (Digital Commons); CONTENTdm

Digital preservation strategy: digital preservation services under discussion; OCLC digital archive; local storage; magnetic tape

Additional services: graphic design (print or web); training; analytics; cataloging; metadata; open URL support contract/license preparation; author copyright advisory; digitization; image services; hosting of supplemental content

ADDITIONAL INFORMATION
Plans for expansion/future directions: Adding older materials and building a robust service to gather and publish faculty works.

HIGHLIGHTED PUBLICATION

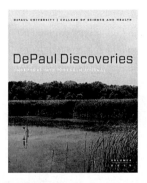

DePaul Discoveries is a peer-reviewed undergraduate research journal published by DePaul University's College of Science and Health.

via.library.depaul.edu/depaul-disc

DUKE UNIVERSITY
Duke University Libraries

Primary Unit: Office of Copyright and Scholarly Communications
scholarworks@duke.edu

Primary Contact: Paolo Mangiafico
Coordinator of Scholarly Communications Technology
919-613-6317
paolo.mangiafico@duke.edu

Website: library.duke.edu/research/openaccess

Social media: @DukeOpenAccess

PROGRAM OVERVIEW

Mission statement: Duke University Libraries partners with members of the Duke community to publish and disseminate scholarship in new and creative ways, including helping to publish scholarly journals on an open access digital platform, archiving previously published and original works, and consulting on new forms of scholarly dissemination.

Year publishing activities began: 2007

Organization: services are distributed across library units/departments

Total FTE in support of publishing activities: professional staff (1)

Funding sources (%): library operating budget (100)

PUBLISHING ACTIVITIES

Library publications in 2015: campus-based faculty-driven journals (4); technical/research reports (10); databases (2); ETDs (500); undergraduate capstones/honors theses (40); research blogs; digital scholarship projects; curated archival collections.

Media formats: text; images; audio; video; data; concept maps, modeling, maps, or other visualizations; multimedia/interactive content

Disciplinary specialties: Greek, Roman, and Byzantine studies; transatlantic German studies; 18th-century Russian studies; cultural anthropology; philosophy

Top publications: *Cultural Anthropology* (journal); *Greek, Roman, and Byzantine Studies* (journal); *Andererseits* (journal); *Vivliofika* (journal); *Project Vox* (scholarly website)

Percentage of journals that are peer reviewed: 100

Internal partners: campus departments or programs; individual faculty; graduate students; undergraduate students

External partners: Society for Cultural Anthropology; editors of particular journals and their organizations

Publishing platform(s): DSpace; Fedora; Hydra; OJS; WordPress; Omeka;

Digital preservation strategy: Archive-It; CLOCKSS; LOCKSS; Portico; in-house; digital preservation services under discussion

Additional services: outreach; training; analytics; cataloging; metadata; notification of A&I sources; ISSN registry; DOI assignment/allocation of identifiers; open URL support; dataset management; author copyright advisory; other author advisory; digitization; data visualization; hosting of supplemental content

ADDITIONAL INFORMATION
Plans for expansion/future directions: Working with more datasets, digital projects, and forms other than linear text; exploring platforms that support new publishing models, not just digital versions of old journal models. Providing more consulting services to members of our community on appropriate tools and venues for publishing their work online, whether or not on a library-hosted platform.

EAST CAROLINA UNIVERSITY
Joyner Library

Primary Unit: Research and Scholarly Communication
scholarlycomm@ecu.edu

Primary Contact: Jeanne Hoover
Scholarly Communication Librarian
252-328-2261
hooverj@ecu.edu

Website: lib.ecu.edu/scholcomm

PROGRAM OVERVIEW
Mission statement: Our primary publishing activity is to make available our institution's electronic theses and dissertations. We also make available gray literature and other student papers (such as honors theses and capstone papers).

Year publishing activities began: 2009

Organization: services are distributed across library units/departments

Total FTE in support of publishing activities: professional staff (0.25); paraprofessional staff (0.5); graduate students (0.5)

Funding sources (%): library operating budget (100)

PUBLISHING ACTIVITIES
Library publications in 2015: technical/research reports (5); faculty conference papers and proceedings (5); ETDs (300); undergraduate capstones/honors theses (70)

Media formats: text; images; audio; video; data

Internal partners: campus departments or programs; individual faculty; graduate students; undergraduate students

Publishing platform(s): DSpace

Digital preservation strategy: in-house

Additional services: cataloging; metadata

ADDITIONAL INFORMATION

Plans for expansion/future directions: Interest in expanding to OJS and OER (perhaps hosted in OMP).

EMBRY-RIDDLE AERONAUTICAL UNIVERSITY
Hunt Library/Hazy Library

Primary Unit: Hunt Library
commons@erau.edu

Primary Contact: Chip Wolfe
Digitization Specialist
386-226-7369
wolfe309@erau.edu

PROGRAM OVERVIEW
Mission statement: ERAU Scholarly Commons is an open access digital repository of the intellectual output produced by the faculty, students, and staff of Embry-Riddle Aeronautical University. By collecting and preserving the University community's research in a single location, ERAU Scholarly Commons provides a digital showcase for campus publications, archival materials, library special collections, and other University-related creative works not published elsewhere.

Year publishing activities began: 2013

Organization: services are distributed across several campuses

Total FTE in support of publishing activities: professional staff (2); paraprofessional staff (0.75); undergraduate students (1)

Funding sources (%): library operating budget (46); non-library campus budget (54)

PUBLISHING ACTIVITIES
Library publications in 2015: campus-based faculty-driven journals (2); campus-based student-driven journals (1); monographs (1); technical/research reports (20); faculty conference papers and proceedings (550); student conference papers and proceedings (40); ETDs (323)

Media formats: text; images; audio; video; data

Disciplinary specialties: aerospace; aviation; aeronautics; airline quality; unmanned aircraft systems

Top publications: *Journal of Aviation/Aerospace Education and Research* (journal); *Space Congress Proceedings* (conference proceedings); *Airline Quality Rating Report* (technical reports); *International Journal of Aviation, Aeronautics, and Aerospace* (journal); *Avion* (newspaper)

Percentage of journals that are peer reviewed: 75

Internal partners: campus departments or programs; individual faculty; graduate students; undergraduate students

External partners: Canaveral Council of Technical Societies

Publishing platform(s): bepress (Digital Commons)

Digital preservation strategy: in-house; Iron Mountain

Additional services: graphic design (print or web); training; analytics; metadata; ISSN registry; DOI assignment/allocation of identifiers; author copyright advisory; other author advisory; digitization; audio/video streaming

ADDITIONAL INFORMATION
Plans for expansion/future directions: The Hunt Library plans to hire a Scholarly Communications Librarian dedicated full time to the open access publishing needs of the university.

EMORY UNIVERSITY
Emory University Library

Primary Unit: Emory Center for Digital Scholarship
ecds@emory.edu

Primary Contact: Sarah Melton
Digital projects coordinator
404-312-3517
smelton@emory.edu

Website: digitalscholarship.emory.edu

Social media: @EmoryCDS

PROGRAM OVERVIEW
Mission statement: The Emory Center for Digital Scholarship (ECDS) conceives of publication broadly. Our publication program takes diverse forms, including journals, blogs and magazines, 3-D visualizations, datasets, GIS projects, and in-house developed applications for reading and disseminating scholarly content. ECDS is committed to open access publishing and digital scholarship that engages both academic and popular audiences. The Scholarly Communications Office manages the open access repositories OpenEmory and ETDs for the scholarly works of Emory faculty and students.

Year publishing activities began: 1994

Organization: services are distributed across campus

Total FTE in support of publishing activities: professional staff (4); graduate students (8)

Funding sources (%): library operating budget (95); grants (5)

PUBLISHING ACTIVITIES
Library publications in 2015: campus-based faculty-driven journals (4); campus-based student-driven journals (2); databases (18); ETDs (695)

Media formats: text; images; audio; video; data; concept maps, modeling, maps, or other visualizations; multimedia/interactive content

Disciplinary specialties: Southern studies; religious studies; medical humanities; Atlanta studies

Top publications: *Southern Spaces* (journal); *Molecular Vision* (journal); *Atlanta Studies* (journal and website); *Practical Matters* (journal); *Sacred Matters* (journal)

Percentage of journals that are peer reviewed: 100

Internal partners: campus departments or programs; individual faculty; graduate students; undergraduate students

Publishing platform(s): Fedora; OJS; OCS; OMP; WordPress; locally developed software; Drupal

Digital preservation strategy: Amazon S3; MetaArchive; digital preservation services under discussion

Additional services: graphic design (print or web); copy-editing; outreach; training; analytics; metadata; dataset management; budget preparation; contract/license preparation; author copyright advisory; digitization; image services; data visualization; hosting of supplemental content; audio/video streaming; consulting on long-term archiving; consulting on indexing

ADDITIONAL INFORMATION
Plans for expansion/future directions: ECDS is currently developing a suite of open source publication tools that we plan to release in the upcoming few years. In particular, we have developed a set of Drupal modules that other journals interested in using Drupal as a platform can use as a basis. We also have released an open source application for creating mobile tours, and we are in the process of developing a platform for annotating scholarly texts, as well as a platform for collaborative mapping.

HIGHLIGHTED PUBLICATION

Southern Spaces
ABOUT   EDITORS   SUBMIT   CONTACT   LOGIN

BLACK LIVES MATTER

Contesting the Roadways: The Moore's Ford Lynching Reenactment and a Confederate Flag Rally, July 25, 2015   MARK AUSLANDER

BLOG POST

A peer-reviewed, multimedia, open access journal about the spaces and places of the US South and their global connections.

southernspaces.org

FLORIDA INTERNATIONAL UNIVERSITY
University Libraries

Primary Unit: Digital Collections Center
dcc@fiu.edu

Primary Contact: Jill Krefft
Institutional Repository Coordinator
jkrefft@fiu.edu

Website: digitalcommons.fiu.edu

PROGRAM OVERVIEW
Mission statement: FIU's Institutional Repository is a full-text, online, open access repository and publishing platform for the scholarship and creative output of FIU. The goals of the repository are to serve as a persistent and centralized access point for FIU scholarship and creative works; promote faculty and student research to a global community; and preserve the history, growth, and development of FIU. The mission of the Florida International University publishing program is to provide a set of services and tools to host, provide open access to, and preserve research and scholarship created by members of FIU.

Year publishing activities began: 2009

Organization: centralized library publishing unit/department

Total FTE in support of publishing activities: professional staff (1.5); paraprofessional staff (1)

Funding sources (%): library operating budget (100)

PUBLISHING ACTIVITIES
Library publications in 2015: campus-based faculty-driven journals (3); campus-based student-driven journals (1); technical/research reports (98); faculty conference papers and proceedings (90); student conference papers and proceedings (22); newsletters (5); ETDs (1922); undergraduate capstones/honors theses (66); working papers (91); occasional papers (69)

Media formats: text; images; video

Disciplinary specialties: education; environmental sciences; history; health and medical administration; biology

Top publications: ETDs; *Hospitality Review* (journal); *South Florida Education Research Conference Proceedings* (conference proceedings); *Class, Race and Corporate Power* (journal); Florida International University Course Catalogs

Percentage of journals that are peer reviewed: 50

Internal partners: campus departments or programs; individual faculty; graduate students; undergraduate students

Publishing platform(s): bepress (Digital Commons)

Digital preservation strategy: Florida Digital Archive (FDA) - FLVC

Additional services: outreach; training; analytics; metadata ISSN registry; peer review management; digitization; image services; hosting of supplemental content

ADDITIONAL INFORMATION

Plans for expansion/future directions: Work with faculty and students for hosting data associated with research. Include more student works and students publications.

FLORIDA STATE UNIVERSITY
Robert Manning Strozier Library

Primary Unit: Technology and Digital Scholarship

Primary Contact: Devin Soper
Scholarly Communication Librarian
850-645-2600
dsoper@fsu.edu

Website: www.lib.fsu.edu/drs

PROGRAM OVERVIEW
Mission statement: University Libraries' Office of Digital Research & Scholarship provides consultations and information about open access, as well as FSU's institutional repository, and administration of the Open Access Publishing Fund. The Academic Publishing Team works directly with faculty and students to achieve their academic publishing goals by providing tools and expertise in dissemination of scholarly work, managing copyrights, and maximizing the impacts of research.

Year publishing activities began: 2011

Organization: centralized library publishing unit/department

Total FTE in support of publishing activities: professional staff (1); graduate students (0.25)

Funding sources (%): library operating budget (100)

PUBLISHING ACTIVITIES
Library publications in 2015: campus-based faculty-driven journals (3); campus-based student-driven journals (1); technical/research reports (1); student conference papers and proceedings (50); ETDs (1500); undergraduate capstones/honors theses (100)

Disciplinary specialties: art education; undergraduate research; law; arts and literature

Top publications: *FSU Law Review* (journal); *The Owl: The Florida State University Undergraduate Research Journal* (journal); *Journal of Art for Life* (journal); *HEAL: Humanism Evolving through Arts and Literature* (journal)

Percentage of journals that are peer reviewed: 100

Internal partners: campus departments or programs; individual faculty; graduate students; undergraduate students

Publishing platform(s): Islandora; OJS

Digital preservation strategy: digital preservation services under discussion

Additional services: outreach; training; analytics; metadata; ISSN registry; open URL support; peer review management; business model development; contract/ license preparation; author copyright advisory; other author advisory; hosting of supplemental content

ADDITIONAL INFORMATION

Plans for expansion/future directions: The Office of Digital Research & Scholarship seeks to expand services by: providing support and hosting to new journals and formats, as well as advising and consulting for existing journals; transitioning from our bepress-based IR to one based on Islandora; and supporting the development of OER on campus.

GEORGE FOX UNIVERSITY
George Fox University Libraries

Primary Unit: Technical Services Department
arolfe@georgefox.edu

Primary Contact: Alex Rolfe
Technical Services Librarian and Systems Administrator
503-554-2414
arolfe@georgefox.edu

Website: digitalcommons.georgefox.edu

PROGRAM OVERVIEW
Mission statement: We aim to showcase the intellectual output of George Fox University by making it easily discoverable and, whenever possible, open access. We also provide access to material from our archives and publish three journals: *Quaker Religious Thought, Quaker Studies,* and *Occasional Papers on Religion in Eastern Europe.*

Year publishing activities began: 2010

Organization: services are distributed across library units/departments

Total FTE in support of publishing activities: professional staff (0.5); paraprofessional staff (0.25); undergraduate students (3)

Funding sources (%): library operating budget (100)

PUBLISHING ACTIVITIES
Library publications in 2015: journals produced under contract/MOU for external groups (3); ETDs (235); archival materials; faculty journal articles

Media formats: text; images; audio; video

Disciplinary specialties: Christianity; psychology; business; education

Top publications: *Quaker Studies* (journal); *Occasional Papers on Religion in Eastern Europe; Quaker Religious Thought* (journal); "'Some Worthless and Reckless Fellows': Landlessness and Parasocial Leadership in Judges" (scholarly article); "The Last of the Rephaim: Conquest and Cataclysm in the Heroic Ages of Ancient Israel" (thesis or dissertation); "The Science of Running: Factors Contributing to Injury Rates in Shod and Unshod Populations" (scholarly article)

Percentage of journals that are peer reviewed: 33

Internal partners: campus departments or programs; individual faculty; graduate students

External partners: Quaker Theological Discussion Group; Woodbrooke Quaker Study Centre

Publishing platform(s): bepress (Digital Commons)

Digital preservation strategy: bepress (Digital Commons)

Additional services: outreach; training; analytics; cataloging; metadata; author copyright advisory; digitization; hosting of supplemental content; audio/video streaming

GEORGE MASON UNIVERSITY
University Libraries

Primary Unit: Mason Publishing
publish@gmu.edu

Primary Contact: Wally Grotophorst
Associate University Librarian
703-993-9005
wallyg@gmu.edu

Website: publishing.gmu.edu

PROGRAM OVERVIEW
Mission statement: Mason Publishing combines a robust digital library publishing program with the George Mason University Press to provide a full range of scholarly publishing services to the university.

Year publishing activities began: 2009

Organization: centralized library publishing unit/department

Total FTE in support of publishing activities: professional staff (4); graduate students (1)

Funding sources (%): library operating budget (90); charitable contributions/ Friends of the Library organizations (5); sales revenue (5)

PUBLISHING ACTIVITIES
Library publications in 2015: campus-based faculty-driven journals (4); campus-based student-driven journals (1); newsletters (2); ETDs (444); Oral histories (27)

Media formats: text; images; audio; video; data

Top publications: *Philosophy & Public Policy Quarterly* (journal); *Journal of Mason Graduate Research* (journal); *New Voices in Public Policy* (journal); "PLASMA: Combining Predicate Logic and Probability for Information Fusion and Decision Support" (scholarly article)

Percentage of journals that are peer reviewed: 100

Internal partners: campus departments or programs; individual faculty; graduate students; undergraduate students

University press partners: University of Virginia Press

Publishing platform(s): DSpace; OJS; WordPress; Luna Imaging

Digital preservation strategy: Amazon S3; CLOCKSS; LOCKSS; Portico

Additional services: graphic design (print or web); print-on-demand; typesetting; copy-editing; ISSN registry; dataset management; author copyright advisory; other author advisory; digitization; hosting of supplemental content

ADDITIONAL INFORMATION
Plans for expansion/future directions: Data publishing

GEORGETOWN UNIVERSITY
Georgetown University Library

Primary Unit: Library Information Technology (LIT)
digitalscholarship@georgetown.edu

Primary Contact: Kate Dohe
Digital Services Librarian
202-687-6387
kd602@georgetown.edu

Website: www.library.georgetown.edu/digitalgeorgetown

Social media: @gtownlibrary

PROGRAM OVERVIEW
Mission statement: DigitalGeorgetown supports the advancement of education and scholarship at Georgetown and contributes to the expansion of research initiatives, both nationally and internationally. By providing the infrastructure, resources, and services, DigitalGeorgetown sustains the evolution from the traditional research models of today to the enriched scholarly communication environment of tomorrow, and it provides context and leadership in developing collaborative opportunities with partners across the campus and around the world.

Year publishing activities began: 2009

Organization: centralized library publishing unit/department

Total FTE in support of publishing activities: professional staff (0.5); undergraduates (0.5)

Funding sources (%): library operating budget (100)

PUBLISHING ACTIVITIES
Library publications in 2015: campus-based student-driven journals (4); faculty conference papers and proceedings (1); newsletters (2); ETDs (275); undergraduate capstones/honors theses (18)

Media formats: text; images; audio; video; data; concept maps, modeling, maps, or other visualizations

Disciplinary specialties: linguistics; communications; international relations/foreign policy; bioethics; public policy

Top publications: *IMF and the Third World: Will the Cure Kill?* (video); *Human Dignity and Bioethics: Essays Commissioned by the President's Council on Bioethics* (anthology); *The Negative Impact of the One Child Policy on the Chinese Society as it Relates to the Parental* (thesis or dissertation); *Clinical Ethics: A Practical Approach to Ethical Decisions in Clinical Medicine* (textbook); *Defining Death* (white paper)

Percentage of journals that are peer reviewed: 100

Internal partners: campus departments or programs; individual faculty; graduate students; undergraduate students

University press partners: Georgetown University Press

Publishing platform(s): DSpace

Digital preservation strategy: in-house; APTrust members

Additional services: marketing; outreach; training; analytics; metadata; author copyright advisory; other author advisory; digitization; image services; audio/video streaming

ADDITIONAL INFORMATION
Plans for expansion/future directions: We continue to offer new services related to faculty and student publishing as the demand increases. Plans are to work more with faculty and student organizations to increase the number of journals published directly through the repository.

GETTYSBURG COLLEGE
Musselman Library

Primary Unit: Scholarly Communications
jwertzbe@gettysburg.edu

Primary Contact: Janelle Wertzberger
Assistant Dean and Director of Scholarly Communications
717-337-7010
jwertzbe@gettysburg.edu

Website: cupola.gettysburg.edu

PROGRAM OVERVIEW
Mission statement: Our publishing mission is to increase visibility of and access to the scholarly works and creative activities of Gettysburg College faculty, students, and staff.

Year publishing activities began: 2012

Organization: centralized library publishing unit/department

Total FTE in support of publishing activities: professional staff (0.25); undergraduates (0.2)

Funding sources (%): library operating budget (90); grants (10)

PUBLISHING ACTIVITIES
Library publications in 2015: campus-based student-driven journals (4); journals produced under contract/MOU for external groups (1); monographs (13); textbooks (1); newsletters (3); databases (1); undergraduate capstones/honors theses (92); images of student studio art; student assignments and presentations; previously published faculty articles and book chapters

Media formats: text; images; audio; video; data; multimedia/interactive content

Disciplinary specialties: U.S. Civil War; history; computer science; library science

Top publications: *You've Gotta Read This! Summer Readers at Musselman Library* (anthology); *Digital Circuit Projects* (OER); *The Gettysburg Historical Journal* (journal); *The Gettysburg College Journal of the Civil War Era* (journal); Schmucker Art Gallery Catalogs

Percentage of journals that are peer reviewed: 60

Internal partners: campus departments or programs; individual faculty; undergraduate students

External partners: Adams County Historical Society

Publishing platform(s): bepress (Digital Commons); CONTENTdm; WordPress; Shared Shelf

Digital preservation strategy: Archive-It; in-house

Additional services: graphic design (print or web); outreach; training; cataloging; metadata; ISSN registry; peer review management; author copyright advisory; digitization; hosting of supplemental content

ADDITIONAL INFORMATION

Plans for expansion/future directions: Increase support for student-edited journals. Encourage creation and sharing of OERs.

GRAND VALLEY STATE UNIVERSITY
Grand Valley State University Libraries

FOUNDER

Primary Unit: Collections and Scholarly Communications
scholarworks@gvsu.edu

Primary Contact: Jacklyn Rander
Publishing Services Manager
616-331-2623
randerja@gvsu.edu

Website: scholarworks.gvsu.edu

PROGRAM OVERVIEW
Mission statement: We provide a platform and support for the publication of scholarly, educational, and creative works affiliated with GVSU, including journals, open education materials, conference sites/proceedings, and ETDs.

Year publishing activities began: 2008

Organization: centralized library publishing unit/department

Total FTE in support of publishing activities: professional staff (2); paraprofessional staff (0.75)

Funding sources (%): library operating budget (100)

PUBLISHING ACTIVITIES
Library publications in 2015: campus-based faculty-driven journals (7); campus-based student-driven journals (6); textbooks (1); technical/research reports (1); ETDs (57); undergraduate capstones/honors theses (48)

Media formats: text; images; video; data

Disciplinary specialties: psychology; philanthropy; history; education; tourism

Top publications: *Online Readings in Psychology and Culture* (journal); *Language Arts Journal of Michigan* (journal); *Journal of Tourism Insights* (journal); *The Foundation Review* (journal); *College Student Affairs Leadership Journal* (journal)

Percentage of journals that are peer reviewed: 65

Internal partners: campus departments or programs; individual faculty; graduate students; undergraduate students

External partners: Michigan Council of Teachers of English; Resort and Commercial Recreation Association; International Association for Cross-Cultural Psychology; Johnson Center for Philanthropy

Publishing platform(s): bepress (Digital Commons)

Digital preservation strategy: Amazon Glacier; LOCKSS; Portico; digital preservation services under discussion

Additional services: outreach; training; analytics; cataloging; metadata; notification of A&I sources; ISSN registry; DOI assignment/allocation of identifiers; dataset management; author copyright advisory; digitization; hosting of supplemental content

HIGHLIGHTED PUBLICATION

Online Readings in Psychology and Culture (ORPC) serves as a resource for researchers, teachers, students, and anyone interested in the interrelationships between psychology and culture. As part of the IACCP, this publication is a free resource for readers and authors.

scholarworks.gvsu.edu/orpc

GUSTAVUS ADOLPHUS COLLEGE
Folke Bernadotte Memorial Library

Primary Unit: Library

Primary Contact: Barbara Fister
Academic Librarian
507-933-7553
fister@gac.edu

PROGRAM OVERVIEW
Mission statement: We hope to explore (with faculty in the disciplines) alternatives to closed access publishing systems.

Year publishing activities began: 2012

Organization: We're so small (6 librarians, one of whom is also the college archivist) that we wear many hats, including this one. If I had to characterize it in a word, I would call it "anarchist."

Funding sources (%): library materials budget (100)

PUBLISHING ACTIVITIES
Library publications in 2015: We expect to do more digital humanities projects that will be public in the next few years.

Media formats: text; images

Internal partners: individual faculty

External partners: Oberlin Group; we also kick in some support for an OA LIS journal

Publishing platform(s): PressBooks

Digital preservation strategy: in-house

Additional services: cataloging

ADDITIONAL INFORMATION

Plans for expansion/future directions: We are among Oberlin Group libraries involved in planning the Leaver Initiative, an open access monograph press focusing on the liberal arts (leverinitiative.wordpress.com). We also are planning to set aside a percentage of our acquisitions budget annually to devote to OA support. At the moment it's a *very tiny* percentage, but we hope it's a way to be intentional about our commitment to sharing knowledge with the world.

ILLINOIS WESLEYAN UNIVERSITY
The Ames Library

Primary Unit: Scholarly Communications

Primary Contact: Stephanie Davis-Kahl
Scholarly Communications Librarian
309-556-3010
sdaviska@iwu.edu

PROGRAM OVERVIEW
Mission statement: The Ames Library publishing program focuses on disseminating excellent student-authored and peer reviewed research, scholarship, and creative works, with an emphasis on providing education and outreach on issues related to publishing such as Open Access, author rights, and copyright.

Year publishing activities began: 2008

Organization: centralized library publishing unit/department

Total FTE in support of publishing activities: professional staff (1); paraprofessional staff (1); undergraduate students (2)

Funding sources (%): library operating budget (25); non-library campus budget (75)

PUBLISHING ACTIVITIES
Library publications in 2015: campus-based student-driven journals (8); student conference papers and proceedings (2); newsletters (1); undergraduate capstones/honors theses (26)

Media formats: text; images; audio; video

Disciplinary specialties: economics; political science; history

Top publications: *Undergraduate Economic Review* (journal); *Constructing History* (journal); *Res Publica* (journal)

Percentage of journals that are peer reviewed: 100

Internal partners: campus departments or programs; individual faculty; undergraduate students

Publishing platform(s): bepress (Digital Commons)

Digital preservation strategy: in-house; digital preservation services under discussion

Additional services: training; analytics; metadata; peer review management; author copyright advisory; other author advisory; hosting of supplemental content; audio/video streaming

ADDITIONAL INFORMATION
Plans for expansion/future directions: We continue to seek out ways to position the program to become a publishing outlet for faculty.

INDIANA UNIVERSITY
Indiana University Libraries

Primary Unit: IUScholarWorks
iusw@indiana.edu

Primary Contact: Shayna Pekala
Scholarly Communication Librarian
812-855-7769
spekala@indiana.edu

Website: scholarworks.iu.edu

PROGRAM OVERVIEW
Mission statement: IUScholarWorks is a set of services provided by the Indiana University Libraries to make the work of IU scholars freely available and to ensure that these resources are preserved and organized for the future.

Year publishing activities began: 2006

Organization: services are distributed across library units/departments

Total FTE in support of publishing activities: professional staff (2.5); graduate students (.25); undergraduates (.25)

Funding sources (%): library materials budget (5); library operating budget (90); endowment income (5)

PUBLISHING ACTIVITIES
Library publications in 2015: campus-based faculty-driven journals (19); campus-based student-driven journals (5); monographs (92); technical/research reports (332); newsletters (10); ETDs (565)

Media formats: text; images; audio; video; data; multimedia/interactive content

Disciplinary specialties: folklore

Top publications: *Journal of the Scholarship of Teaching and Learning* (journal); *Indiana Magazine of History* (journal); *Textual Cultures* (journal); *Museum Anthropology Review* (journal); *The Medieval Review* (journal)

Percentage of journals that are peer reviewed: 90

Internal partners: campus departments or programs; individual faculty; graduate students; undergraduate students

External partners: American Folklore Society

University press partners: IU Press

Publishing platform(s): DSpace; OJS

Digital preservation strategy: AP Trust; Archive-It; CLOCKSS; DuraCloud; DPN; HathiTrust; LOCKSS; Portico

Additional services: outreach; training; analytics; cataloging; metadata; notification of A&I sources; ISSN registry; DOI assignment/allocation of identifiers; dataset management; peer review management; author copyright advisory; digitization; image services; data visualization; hosting of supplemental content; audio/video streaming

ADDITIONAL INFORMATION

Plans for expansion/future directions: Incorporating the Libraries' open access publishing activities into the development of a new campus office, the Office of Scholarly Publishing, which includes the University Press and an eTextbook initiative.

INDIANA UNIVERSITY
PURDUE UNIVERSITY INDIANAPOLIS (IUPUI)

Indiana University Purdue University
Indianapolis (IUPUI) University Library

Primary Unit: IUPUI University Library Center for Digital Scholarship
digschol@iupui.edu

Primary Contact: Ted Polley
Social Sciences Librarian
317-274-8552
dapolley@iupui.edu

Website: www.ulib.iupui.edu/digitalscholarship

Social media: @IUPUIDigSchol

PROGRAM OVERVIEW

Mission statement: The IUPUI University Library Center for Digital Scholarship
enriches the research capabilities of scholars at IUPUI, within Indiana
communities, and beyond by: digitally disseminating unique scholarship, data,
and artifacts created by IUPUI faculty, students, staff, and community partners;
advocating for the rights of authors, fair use, and open access to information
and publications; implementing and promoting best practices for creation,
description, preservation, sharing, and reuse of digital scholarship, data, and
artifacts; strategically applying research-supporting technologies; and teaching
digital literacy.

Year publishing activities began: 2007

Organization: services are distributed across library units/departments

Total FTE in support of publishing activities: professional staff (2–3);
paraprofessional staff (3–4)

Funding sources (%): library operating budget (90); grants (10)

PUBLISHING ACTIVITIES

Library publications in 2015: campus-based faculty-driven journals (4); campus-
based student-driven journals (4); journals produced under contract/MOU for
external groups (2); ETDs (308)

Media formats: text; images; audio; video; data

Disciplinary specialties: Indianapolis history; social work; law; science; civics

Top publications: Indianapolis City Directories; *Advances in Social Work* (journal); *Indiana Law Review* (journal); *Proceedings of the Indiana Academy of Science* (journal); *Journal of Civic Literacy* (journal)

Percentage of journals that are peer reviewed: 90

Internal partners: campus departments or programs; individual faculty; graduate students

External partners: Indiana Library Federation; Indiana Teachers of English Speakers of Other Languages; Indiana Academy of Science

Publishing platform(s): CONTENTdm; DSpace; OJS

Digital preservation strategy: DuraCloud; DPN; digital preservation services under discussion; some preservation in DuraCloud

Additional services: training; analytics; cataloging; DOI assignment/allocation of identifiers; open URL support; dataset management; author copyright advisory; digitization

ADDITIONAL INFORMATION
Plans for expansion/future directions: At present we support the technologies that allow for open access publishing (DSpace, OJS) as well as training on these technologies and some general limited support regarding how to start a new journal. We have discussed fuller support of the editorial/publishing process through provision of copy editing and journal/issue formatting support. We expect to use DPN for digital preservation once it's realized.

IOWA STATE UNIVERSITY
Iowa State University Library

Primary Unit: Digital Repository
digirep@iastate.edu

Primary Contact: Harrison W. Inefuku
Digital Repository Coordinator
515-294-3180
hinefuku@iastate.edu

Website: lib.dr.iastate.edu

PROGRAM OVERVIEW
Mission statement: Digital Repository @ Iowa State University provides free public access to research, scholarship, and creative works by Iowa State's faculty, students, and staff, increasing visibility and impact and supporting our university's land-grant mission. We provide support and hosting for publishing peer-reviewed journals, conference proceedings, and monographs.

Year publishing activities began: 2012

Organization: centralized library publishing unit/department

Total FTE in support of publishing activities: professional staff (2.6); paraprofessional staff (2); undergraduate students (1)

Funding sources (%): library operating budget (50); non-library campus budget (50)

PUBLISHING ACTIVITIES
Library publications in 2015: campus-based student-driven journals (1); ETDs (15,851); conference proceedings (3)

Media formats: text; images; audio; video; data

Top publications: *Journal of Critical Thought and Praxis* (journal); *Review of Progress in Quantitative Nondestructive Evaluation* (journal)

Percentage of journals that are peer reviewed: 100

Internal partners: campus departments or programs; individual faculty; graduate students; undergraduate students

External partners: Alliance for the Arts in Research Universities (a2ru)

Publishing platform(s): bepress (Digital Commons)

Digital preservation strategy: digital preservation services under discussion

Additional services: marketing; outreach; training; analytics; cataloging; metadata; ISSN registry; peer review management; author copyright advisory; other author advisory; digitization; hosting of supplemental content; audio/video streaming

ADDITIONAL INFORMATION
Plans for expansion/future directions: Continuing to support our faculty, students, and staff to increase the visibility and impact of their research and scholarship through open access. Expanding our journal and conference proceedings publication activities.

JAMES MADISON UNIVERSITY
JMU Libraries and Educational Technologies

Primary Unit: Collections
lib-digitalcollections@jmu.edu

Primary Contact: Laura Drake Davis
Digital Collections Librarian
540-568-4086
davisld@jmu.edu

Website: commons.lib.jmu.edu

PROGRAM OVERVIEW
Mission statement: The purpose of Library & Educational Technologies' publishing program is to provide a central hub for scholarship associated with James Madison University. By providing this space, we enable: the discovery of research; platforms for open access and non-traditional publications; a survey of the local research landscape; and the identification of collaborators for future research. While the program at James Madison University is new, the anticipated publishing scope is broad and includes journals, conference proceedings, ETDs, and select Special Collections materials. It is anticipated that additional material types will be added, including datasets, campus publications, and other campus-produced materials.

Year publishing activities began: 2013

Organization: centralized library publishing unit/department

Total FTE in support of publishing activities: professional staff (1); paraprofessional staff (1.5)

Funding sources (%): library operating budget (100)

PUBLISHING ACTIVITIES
Library publications in 2015: campus-based student-driven journals (2); student conference papers and proceedings (1); ETDs (126); undergraduate capstones/honors theses (118)

Media formats: text; images; audio; video; data; concept maps, modeling, maps, or other visualizations

Percentage of journals that are peer reviewed: 100

Internal partners: campus departments or programs; individual faculty; graduate students; undergraduate students

Publishing platform(s): bepress (Digital Commons); WordPress; locally developed software

Digital preservation strategy: LOCKSS; Portico; digital preservation services under discussion

Additional services: marketing; outreach; training; analytics; cataloging; metadata; dataset management; other author advisory; digitization; audio/video streaming

JOHNS HOPKINS UNIVERSITY
Sheridan Libraries

Primary Unit: Scholarly Resources and Special Collections
etd-support@jhu.edu

Primary Contact: David Reynolds
Manager of Scholarly Digital Initiatives
410-516-7220
davidr@jhu.edu

Website: jscholarship.library.jhu.edu

PROGRAM OVERVIEW
Mission statement: To provide a publishing platform for required ETDs and journals for the Johns Hopkins academic community.

Year publishing activities began: 2009

Organization: services are distributed across library units/departments

Total FTE in support of publishing activities: professional staff (3)

Funding sources (%): library operating budget (80); non-library campus budget (20)

PUBLISHING ACTIVITIES
Library publications in 2015: campus-based faculty-driven journals (2); technical/research reports (20); faculty conference papers and proceedings (20); databases (4); ETDs (750)

Media formats: text; images; audio; data; concept maps, modeling, maps, or other visualizations

Disciplinary specialties: education

Top publications: *International Journal of Interdisciplinary Education* (journal); *New Horizons for Learning* (journal)

Percentage of journals that are peer reviewed: 50

Internal partners: campus departments or programs; individual faculty; graduate students

University press partners: Johns Hopkins University Press

Publishing platform(s): DSpace; OJS; OCS

Digital preservation strategy: HathiTrust; in-house; digital preservation services under discussion

Additional services: training; cataloging; metadata; ISSN registry; open URL support; dataset management; peer review management; author copyright advisory; digitization; image services; hosting of supplemental content

KANSAS STATE UNIVERSITY
Kansas State University Libraries

Primary Unit: Center for Digital Scholarship and Publishing
nppress@ksu.edu

Primary Contact: Char Simser
Coordinator of Electronic Publishing
785-532-7444
nppress@ksu.edu

Website: newprairiepress.org

Social media: @NewPrairiePress

PROGRAM OVERVIEW
Mission statement: To host peer-reviewed scholarly journals, monographs, conference proceedings, and special publications; make the content freely available worldwide; and contribute to and support evolving scholarly publishing models.

Year publishing activities began: 2007

Organization: centralized library publishing unit/department

Total FTE in support of publishing activities: professional staff (1); paraprofessional staff (0.5)

Funding sources (%): library operating budget (100)

PUBLISHING ACTIVITIES
Library publications in 2015: campus-based faculty-driven journals (5); monographs (3); journals produced under contract/external (2); textbooks (1); technical/research reports (106); faculty conference papers and proceedings (108); ETDs (1,161); undergraduate capstones/honors theses (5)

Media formats: text; images; audio; video; concept maps, modeling, maps, or other visualizations

Disciplinary specialties: financial therapy; rural research and policy; library science; literature; cognitive sciences and semantics

Top publications: *Baltic International Yearbook of Cognition, Logic and Communication* (journal); *Journal of Financial Therapy* (journal); *Studies in 20th & 21st Century Literature* (journal); *Online Journal of Rural Research & Policy* (journal); *GDR Bulletin* (journal)

Percentage of journals that are peer reviewed: 100

Internal partners: campus departments or programs; individual faculty; graduate students

External partners: College & University Libraries Section of Kansas Library Association; Center for Cognitive Sciences and Semantics at the University of Latvia

Publishing platform(s): bepress (Digital Commons); DSpace; Omeka

Digital preservation strategy: CLOCKSS; DPN; LOCKSS; Portico

Additional services: graphic design (print or web); marketing; training; notification of A&I sources; ISSN registry; ISBN registry; DOI assignment/allocation of identifiers; digitization; hosting of supplemental content; audio/video streaming

ADDITIONAL INFORMATION

Plans for expansion/future directions: In 2015, we established a Center for Digital Scholarship and Publishing that will include journal, ebook, and conference proceedings publishing services, data services, institutional repository, and continued outreach; we plan to add new journals, conference events, and monographs. Our plans for expansion are in line with the University's strategic directions.

HIGHLIGHTED PUBLICATION

Crossing Borders: An Interdisciplinary Journal of Undergraduate Scholarship seeks to encourage interdisciplinary research among undergraduate students at Kansas State University and elsewhere.

newprairiepress.org/crossingborders

LINFIELD COLLEGE
Jereld R. Nicholson Library

Primary Unit: Collections Management
digitalcommons@linfield.edu

Primary Contact: Kathleen Spring
Collections Management Librarian/DigitalCommons Coordinator
503-883-2263
kspring@linfield.edu

Website: digitalcommons.linfield.edu

Social media: facebook.com/Linfield Libraries; @linlibraries; instagram.com
/linlibraries

PROGRAM OVERVIEW
Mission statement: DigitalCommons@Linfield promotes the discovery, sharing, and preservation of the intellectual and creative works of the faculty, students, and staff of Linfield College, as well as the history and development of the College.

Year publishing activities began: 2010

Organization: centralized library publishing unit/department

Total FTE in support of publishing activities: professional staff (0.3); undergraduate students (3–4 students; 10 hrs./wk.)

Funding sources (%): library operating budget (90); grants (10)

PUBLISHING ACTIVITIES
Library publications in 2015: campus-based student-driven journals (1); newsletters (1); undergraduate capstones/honors theses (16); undergraduate symposium posters; images from art exhibits; archive materials from the Oregon Wine History Archive; alumni magazine

Media formats: text; images; audio; video; data

Disciplinary specialties: undergraduate research; art and visual culture; Oregon wine; Pacific City Dory Fleet

Top publications: Oregon Wine History Archive (digital collection); Linfield College Student Scholarship Symposium (conference abstracts and posters); *Linfield Magazine* (alumni publication); Launching through the Surf: The Dory Fleet of Pacific City (digital collection)

Percentage of journals that are peer reviewed: 100

Internal partners: campus departments or programs; individual faculty; undergraduate students

Publishing platform(s): bepress (Digital Commons)

Digital preservation strategy: in-house; digital preservation services under discussion

Additional services: outreach; training; analytics; author copyright advisory; other author advisory; digitization; image services; hosting of supplemental content; audio/video streaming

LOYOLA UNIVERSITY CHICAGO
Loyola University Chicago Libraries

Primary Unit: Library Systems
ecommons@luc.edu

Primary Contact: Margaret Heller
Digital Services Librarian
773-508-2686
mheller1@luc.edu

Website: ecommons.luc.edu

PROGRAM OVERVIEW
Mission statement: Loyola eCommons is an open-access, sustainable, and secure resource created to preserve and provide access to research, scholarship, and creative works produced by the university community for the benefit of Loyola students, faculty, staff, and the larger academic community. Sponsored by the University Libraries, Loyola eCommons is a suite of online resources, services, and people working in concert to facilitate a wide range of scholarly and archival activities, including collaboration, resource sharing, author rights management, digitization, preservation, and access by a global academic audience.

Year publishing activities began: 2011

Organization: centralized library publishing unit/department

Total FTE in support of publishing activities: professional staff (1); graduate students (.25); undergraduates (1.5)

Funding sources (%): library operating budget (90); non-library campus budget (10)

PUBLISHING ACTIVITIES
Library publications in 2015: campus-based student-driven journals (1); faculty conference papers and proceedings (550); databases (1); ETDs (3000)

Media formats: text; images; video; data

Disciplinary specialties: criminal justice; economics; social work; chemistry; theology

Top publications: "Web 2.0 for reference services staff training and communication" (scholarly article); "Milton's Use of the Epic Simile in Paradise Lost" (thesis or dissertation); "Expressionism in the Plays of Eugene O'Neill" (thesis or dissertation); "Comics and Conflict: War and Patriotically Themed Comics in American Cultural History From World War II Through the Iraq War" (thesis or dissertation); "The Refractive Indices of Ethyl Alcohol and Water Mixtures" (thesis or dissertation)

Internal partners: campus departments or programs; individual faculty; graduate students

Publishing platform(s): bepress (Digital Commons)

Digital preservation strategy: in-house

Additional services: marketing; outreach; training; analytics; author copyright advisory; hosting of supplemental content

ADDITIONAL INFORMATION

Plans for expansion/future directions: We have one journal on its third issue, and another migrating currently.

MACALESTER COLLEGE
DeWitt Wallace Library

Primary Unit: Digital Scholarship & Services
scholarpub@macalester.edu

Primary Contact: Johan Oberg
Digital Scholarship and Services Librarian
651-696-6003
joberg@macalester.edu

Website: www.macalester.edu/library/digitalinitiatives/index.html

Social media: facebook.com/DeWittWallaceLibrary; @MacalesterLib; instagram.com/macalesterlib; macalesterarchives.tumblr.com

PROGRAM OVERVIEW
Mission statement: The Digital Publishing Unit of the DeWitt Wallace Library supports the creation, preservation, and dissemination of local digital-born scholarship in various formats. Essential to supporting this mission is the continued exploration of evolving creation, collaboration, and publication tools; encoding methods; and development of staff skills and facility resources. The Unit serves the digital scholarship and electronic publishing needs through the development of digital scholarship projects as well as open access online distribution of journals, articles, and conference proceedings. The Library is committed to playing an active role in changing the landscape of scholarly publishing and supports the ideals of the open access movement.

Year publishing activities began: 2004

Organization: services are distributed across library units/departments

Total FTE in support of publishing activities: professional staff (1); paraprofessional staff (0.5)

Funding sources (%): library operating budget (100)

PUBLISHING ACTIVITIES
Library publications in 2015: campus-based faculty-driven journals (2); campus-based student-driven journals (2); journals produced under contract/MOU for external groups (1); monographs (1); undergraduate capstones/honors theses (26); oral histories for the college

Media formats: text; images; video; data

Disciplinary specialties: fine arts; humanities; social sciences; natural sciences; interdisciplinary studies

Top publications: *Captive Audiences/Captive Performers* (book chapters); LibTech Conference Presentations; *Himalaya, The Journal of the Association for Nepal and Himalayan Studies* (journal); *Macalester Journal of Physics and Astronomy* (journal); *Tapestries: Interwoven Voices of Local and Global Identities* (journal)

Percentage of journals that are peer reviewed: 100

Internal partners: campus departments or programs; individual faculty; undergraduate students

External partners: Association for Nepal and Himalayan Studies

Publishing platform(s): bepress (Digital Commons); CONTENTdm; WordPress; Omeka

Digital preservation strategy: We have remotely hosted services and we rely on the vendor.

Additional services: graphic design (print or web); typesetting; marketing; outreach; analytics; cataloging; metadata; compiling indexes and/or TOCs; ISSN registry; ISBN registry; dataset management; peer review management; author copyright advisory; other author advisory; digitization; hosting of supplemental content

HIGHLIGHTED PUBLICATION

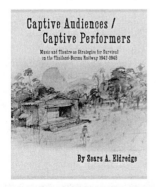

Captive Audiences/Captive Performers tells the story of how music and theatre helped the 61,000 POWs who were sent to Japanese prisoner of war camps in Southeast Asia during World War II survive their ordeal. Taking advantage of the digital platform, the book incorporates audio excerpts and video clips.

digitalcommons.macalester.edu/captiveaudiences

ADDITIONAL INFORMATION

Plans for expansion/future directions: Potential new initiative with Oberlin Group Libraries and Lever Initiative to work on OA monograph publishing. We also recently joined the Open Textbook Network.

MCGILL UNIVERSITY
McGill University Library & Archives

Primary Unit: Digital Initiatives

Primary Contact: Jenn Riley
Associate Dean, Digital Initiatives
514-398-3642
jenn.riley@mcgill.ca

Website: www.mcgill.ca/library/services/scholarly-publishing

PROGRAM OVERVIEW
Mission statement: McGill University Library showcases the research done by the McGill community via publishing initiatives such as electronic theses and dissertations, open access journals and monographs, and by partnering with others to develop new methods to disseminate research.

Year publishing activities began: 1988

Organization: centralized library publishing unit/department

Total FTE in support of publishing activities: professional staff (0.25); paraprofessional staff (0.35); graduate students (0.1)

Funding sources (%): library operating budget (95); grants (5)

PUBLISHING ACTIVITIES
Library publications in 2015: journals produced under contract/MOU for external groups (5); techincal/research reports (56); ETDs (1,031); undergraduate capstones/honors theses (12); The Living Lab (collection of research reports) hosted on behalf of the Office for Sustainability

Media formats: text; images; audio; video

Disciplinary specialties: education; food cultures; library history; cultural issues

Top publications: *McGill Journal of Education* (journal); *CuiZine* (journal); *Fontanus* (journal)

Percentage of journals that are peer reviewed: 90

Internal partners: campus departments or programs; individual faculty; graduate students; undergraduate students

External partners: Public Knowledge Project; Erudit; ThesesCanada

Publishing platform(s): OJS; locally developed software; digitool

Digital preservation strategy: digital preservation services under discussion

Additional services: training; analytics; notification of A&I sources; ISSN registry; ISBN registry; author copyright advisory; digitization; hosting of supplemental content

ADDITIONAL INFORMATION
Plans for expansion/future directions: Data publishing

MCMASTER UNIVERSITY
McMaster University Library

Primary Unit: Sherman Centre for Digital Scholarship
scom@mcmaster.ca

Primary Contact: Gabriela Mircea
Digital Repository Librarian
905-525-9140 x20988
mirceag@mcmaster.ca

Website: library.mcmaster.ca/scholarly-communication

PROGRAM OVERVIEW

Mission statement: The McMaster University Library journal and institutional repository platforms offer state-of-the-art services to the McMaster community. We are strongly committed to using open source software to deliver high-quality services that are both scalable and sustainable.

Year publishing activities began: 2006

Organization: services are distributed across library units/departments

Total FTE in support of publishing activities: professional staff (1.5); undergraduate students (3)

Funding sources (%): library operating budget (100)

PUBLISHING ACTIVITIES

Library publications in 2015: campus-based faculty-driven journals (10); campus-based student-driven journals (8); faculty conference papers and proceedings (55); ETDs (802); undergraduate capstones/honors theses (54)

Media formats: text; images; audio; video; data

Disciplinary specialties: philosophy; literature; communication; health

Top publications: *Early Theatre* (journal); *Russell: The Journal of Bertrand Russell Studies* (journal); *Energy Studies Review* (journal); *Journal of Professional Communication* (journal); *Nexus* (journal)

Percentage of journals that are peer reviewed: 100

Internal partners: campus departments or programs; individual faculty; graduate students; undergraduate students

Publishing platform(s): DSpace; OJS

Digital preservation strategy: in-house; Ontario Library Research Cloud

Additional services: training metadata; DOI assignment/allocation of identifiers; digitization

NORTHEASTERN UNIVERSITY
Northeastern University Library

FOUNDER

Primary Unit: Scholarly Communication and Digital Publishing

Primary Contact: Hillary Corbett
Director, Scholarly Communication and Digital Publishing
617-373-2352
h.corbett@neu.edu

PROGRAM OVERVIEW
Mission statement: Northeastern University Library offers a growing suite of digital publishing services. The library-based publishing program provides an online platform for journal publishing (OJS) and the opportunity to produce innovative online collections and e-books based in its Digital Repository Service (DRS). Through the DRS, the Libraries also provide open access to the university's electronic theses and dissertations, scholarly research output, and university-produced objects. The library also manages the university's partnership with the University Press of New England, which produced titles under the Northeastern University Press (NUP) imprint for 10 years and continues to handle reprints. As part of the publishing program the library will begin creating open-access editions of out-of-print NUP titles in fall 2015.

Year publishing activities began: 2006

Organization: services are distributed across library units/departments

Total FTE in support of publishing activities: professional staff (1); graduate students (0.25); undergraduates (0.25)

Funding sources (%): library operating budget (100)

PUBLISHING ACTIVITIES
Library publications in 2015: campus-based faculty-driven journals (2); campus-based student-driven journals (1); monographs (1); technical/research reports (2); ETDs (334); photographic collections (1); special collections (3)

Media formats: text; images; audio; video; data

Top publications: *Digital Humanities Quarterly* (journal); *Annals of Environmental Science* (journal)

Percentage of journals that are peer reviewed: 100

Internal partners: campus departments or programs; individual faculty; graduate students; undergraduate students

University press partners: University Press of New England

Publishing platform(s): Fedora; Hydra; OJS; WordPress; Issuu

Digital preservation strategy: in-house; digital preservation services under discussion

Additional services: print-on-demand; typesetting; copy-editing; marketing; outreach; training; analytics; metadata; compiling indexes and/or TOCs; notification of A&I sources; ISSN registry; ISBN registry; DOI assignment/allocation of identifiers; dataset management; author copyright advisory; digitization; hosting of supplemental content; audio/video streaming

ADDITIONAL INFORMATION

Plans for expansion/future directions: We are looking forward to our first full year of operating our publishing program in the 2015–2016 academic year. We plan to release open-access digital editions of selected out-of-print Northeastern University Press titles, and create several digital collections of unique materials produced at Northeastern University from our special collections. We also hope to expand usage of Open Journal Systems (OJS) on campus and plan to actively market our journal publishing service.

HIGHLIGHTED PUBLICATION

Annals of Environmental Science publishes original, peer-reviewed research in the environmental sciences, broadly defined. It has been published open-access at Northeastern University since 2007.

www.aes.neu.edu

NORTHWESTERN UNIVERSITY
Northwestern University Libraries

Primary Unit: Center for Scholarly Communication
and Digital Curation
cscdc@northwestern.edu

Primary Contact: John Dorr
Acting Head, Digital Scholarship Services
847-467-1506
john.dorr@northwestern.edu

Website: cscdc.northwestern.edu

Social media: @NU_CSCDC

PROGRAM OVERVIEW
Mission statement: We are engaged in planning activities to identify tools and
support models that enable distributed, preservable publishing projects across the
entire University. In initial phases, we anticipate the emphasis will be heavier on non-
traditional products, particularly digital humanities projects and companion sites.

Year publishing activities began: 2012

Organization: services are distributed across library units/departments

Total FTE in support of publishing activities: professional staff (0.25)

Funding sources (%): library operating budget (100)

PUBLISHING ACTIVITIES
Library-administered university press publications in 2015: journals (1);
monographs (60)

Media formats: text; images; audio; video

Internal partners: individual faculty

University press partners: Northwestern University Press

Publishing platform(s): Fedora; Hydra; WordPress

Digital preservation strategy: DuraCloud; HathiTrust; Hydra; in-house; digital presentation services under discussion

Additional services: author copyright advisory; digitization; image services; hosting of supplemental content

OHIO STATE UNIVERSITY
University Libraries

Primary Unit: Digital Content Services

Primary Contact: Melanie Schlosser
Digital Publishing Librarian
614-688-5877
schlosser.40@osu.edu

Website: library.osu.edu/projectsinitiatives/knowledge-bank

PROGRAM OVERVIEW
Mission statement: Our mission is to engage with partners across the university to increase the amount, value, and impact of OSU-produced digital content.

Year publishing activities began: 2004

Organization: centralized library publishing unit/department

Total FTE in support of publishing activities: professional staff (2.5); undergraduate students (0.25)

Funding sources (%): library operating budget (100)

PUBLISHING ACTIVITIES
Library publications in 2015: campus-based faculty-driven journals (7); journals produced under contract/MOU for external groups (3); monographs (2); textbooks (1); technical/research reports (11); faculty conference papers and proceedings (6); student conference papers and proceedings (9); newsletters (6); undergraduate capstones/honors theses (322); conference and event lectures and presentations (94); graduate student culminating papers and projects (27); graduate student research forum papers and symposia posters (44); undergraduate research forum presentations and posters (71)

Media formats: text; images; audio; video; data

Percentage of journals that are peer reviewed: 100

Internal partners: campus departments or programs; individual faculty; graduate students; undergraduate students

External partners: Society for Disability Studies; Medieval Association of the Midwest; Ohio Academy of Science

Publishing platform(s): DSpace; OJS; WordPress

Digital preservation strategy: digital preservation services under discussion

Additional services: graphic design (print or web); typesetting; training; analytics; cataloging; metadata; compiling indexes and/or TOCs; notification of A&I sources; DOI assignment/allocation of identifiers; contract/license preparation; author copyright advisory; digitization hosting of supplemental content; consulting and educational programming

OREGON STATE UNIVERSITY
Oregon State University Libraries and Press

Primary Unit: Center for Digital Scholarship and Services

FOUNDER

Primary Contact: Michael Boock
Head of the Center for Digital Scholarship and Services
541-737-9155
michael.boock@oregonstate.edu

Website: cdss.library.oregonstate.edu

PROGRAM OVERVIEW
Mission statement: Oregon State University (OSU) Libraries' publishing activities are primarily focused on the dissemination of scholarship produced by OSU faculty and students. This is achieved largely through the institutional repository ScholarsArchive@ OSU, which includes material such as electronic theses and dissertations, agricultural extension reports, conference proceedings, and faculty datasets. OSU Libraries also hosts open access journals that include articles by OSU faculty. The Libraries' Center for Digital Scholarship and Services digitizes selected out-of-print OSU Press publications, and provides open access to excerpts from Press books and supplementary materials such as maps and datasets. OSU Libraries also collaborates with OSU Press and OSU Extended Campus to publish open textbooks by OSU faculty. Other publishing activities involve the development of online resources that present the unique holdings of OSU Libraries, such as the Oregon Hops and Brewing Archives, the Linus and Ava Helen Pauling Papers, and related archival collections in the History of Science.

Year publishing activities began: 2006

Organization: services are distributed across library units/departments

Total FTE in support of publishing activities: professional staff (2); paraprofessional staff (1)

Funding sources (%): library materials budget (80); endowment income (20)

PUBLISHING ACTIVITIES
Library publications in 2015: campus-based faculty-driven journals (1); journals produced under contract/MOU for external groups (1); technical/research reports (50); faculty conference papers and proceedings (200); ETDs (550); undergraduate capstones/honors theses (70); datasets (15)

Media formats: text; images; audio; video; data; multimedia/interactive content

Disciplinary specialties: forestry; agriculture; history of science; water studies

Top publications: "Growing Your Own" (technical report); *Forest Phytophthoras* (journal); *International Institute for Fisheries Economics and Trade Conference Proceedings* (conference proceedings); *Journal of the Transportation Research Forum* (journal); "Reducing Fire Risk on Your Forest Property" (technical report)

Percentage of journals that are peer reviewed: 100

Internal partners: campus departments or programs; individual faculty; graduate students; undergraduate students

External partners: Transportation Research Forum; International Institute for Fisheries Economics and Trade; Western Dry Kiln Association; Oregon Institute for Natural Resources

University press partners: Oregon State University Press

Publishing platform(s): DSpace; Fedora; Hydra; OJS; WordPress

Digital preservation strategy: LOCKSS; MetaArchive

Additional services: graphic design (print or web); analytics; cataloging; metadata; ISSN registry; DOI assignment/allocation of identifiers; dataset management; author copyright advisory; digitization; image services; data visualization; hosting of supplemental content; audio/video streaming

HIGHLIGHTED PUBLICATION

For more than a century, Oregon State University's Extension Service and Agricultural Experiment Station publications have covered everything from winemaking techniques to marine economics.

ir.library.oregonstate.edu/xmlui/handle/1957/3904

ADDITIONAL INFORMATION

Plans for expansion/future directions: Our plans for the near future focus largely on open textbooks, digital humanities, and linking datasets to published articles. The OSU Libraries' Gray Family Chair for Innovative Library Services is developing a strategic vision for digital publishing with an emphasis on platforms that integrate the publishing activities of the Libraries and Press.

PACIFIC UNIVERSITY
Pacific University Libraries

Primary Unit: Local Collections and Publication Services/ Pacific University Press

Primary Contact: Isaac Gilman
Scholarly Communication and Publishing Services Librarian
503-352-1488
gilmani@pacificu.edu

Website: www.pacificu.edu/library/services/lcps/index.cfm; www.pacificu.edu/press

PROGRAM OVERVIEW
Mission statement: Pacific University Libraries' publishing services exist to disseminate diverse and significant scholarly and creative work, regardless of a work's economic potential. Through flexible open access publishing models and author services, Pacific University Libraries will contribute to the discovery of new ideas (from scholars within and outside the Pacific community) and to the sustainability of the publishing system.

Year publishing activities began: 2010

Organization: centralized library publishing unit/department

Total FTE in support of publishing activities: professional staff (0.9); paraprofessional staff (0.1)

Funding sources (%): library operating budget (90); charitable contributions (6); endowment income (4)

PUBLISHING ACTIVITIES
Library publications in 2015: campus-based faculty-driven journals (5); journals produced under contract/MOU for external groups (1); monographs (7); faculty conference papers and proceedings (1); ETDs (44); undergraduate capstones/ honors theses (6)

Media formats: text; images; audio

Disciplinary specialties: health care; philosophy; librarianship

Top publications: *Journal of Librarianship and Scholarly Communication* (journal); *Essays in Philosophy* (journal); *Health & Interprofessional Practice* (journal)

Percentage of journals that are peer reviewed: 86

Internal partners: campus departments or programs; individual faculty

External partners: Oregon Library Association; HELPS International; Society for Study of Occupation:USA

Publishing platform(s): bepress (Digital Commons); Ubiquity Press

Digital preservation strategy: Portico; digital preservation services under discussion

Additional services: print-on-demand; typesetting; copy-editing; marketing; training; analytics; metadata; notification of A&I sources; ISSN registry; ISBN registry; DOI assignment/allocation of identifiers; peer review management; contract/license preparation; author copyright advisory; digitization

ADDITIONAL INFORMATION
Plans for expansion/future directions: With the establishment of the Pacific University Press (2015), our monograph publishing activities will expand over the next 3–5 years; this will include both open access and hybrid access models.

PENNSYLVANIA STATE UNIVERSITY
Pennsylvania State University Libraries

MEMBER INSTITUTION
Library
Publishing
Coalition

FOUNDER

Primary Unit: Publishing & Curation Services
UL-PCS@lists.psu.edu

Primary Contact: Linda Friend
Head, Scholarly Publishing Services
814-865-0673
lxf5@psu.edu

Website: www.libraries.psu.edu/psul/pubcur.html

PROGRAM OVERVIEW
Mission statement: Publishing & Curation Services, a department of the University Libraries, serves the Penn State community of authors and researchers with in-house publishing options and related consultation services. We have a commitment to open access and complement the journal and monograph publishing services of the Penn State University Press, offering practical alternative ways of publishing and disseminating research in many formats using a range of publishing platforms including OJS, OCS, our ScholarSphere repository, WordPress, Omeka, and so forth. We provide assistance to scholarly journals and societies in disseminating their publications and proceedings electronically, and our list includes the three primary journals for Pennsylvania history. Doctoral dissertations and master's theses for most academic programs, as well as the majority of undergraduate honors theses, are submitted digitally and are disseminated through a locally maintained database, and there is an active program of collecting and making other student research available.

Year publishing activities began: 2000

Organization: primarily centralized library publishing unit/department located at the main campus. Various operations and publishing workflow responsibilities and support activities (depending on needs, content, format, etc.) are distributed among a range of library units/departments, including technology support, cataloging and metadata services, digitization and preservation, and so forth.

Total FTE in support of publishing activities: professional staff (2.5); paraprofessional staff (0.75); graduate students (0.25)

Funding sources (%): library operating budget (98); sales revenue (1); licensing revenue (1)

PUBLISHING ACTIVITIES

Library publications in 2015: campus-based faculty-driven journals (6); campus-based student-driven journals (1); journals produced under contract/MOU for external groups (3); faculty conference papers and proceedings (1); ETDs (1400); undergraduate capstones/honors theses (500)

Media formats: text; images; audio; video; data

Disciplinary specialties: Pennsylvania history and culture; digital humanities; philosophy of education

Top publications: *Pennsylvania History* (journal); *Pennsylvania Magazine of History and Biography* (*PMHB*) (journal); *Western Pennsylvania History* (journal); *IK: Other Ways of Knowing* (journal); *Digital Literary Studies* (forthcoming journal)

Percentage of journals that are peer reviewed: 100

Internal partners: campus departments or programs; individual faculty; graduate students; undergraduate students

External partners: Historical Society of Pennsylvania; Heinz History Center; Pennsylvania History Association

University press partners: Penn State University Press

Publishing platform(s): CONTENTdm; Fedora; Hydra; OJS; OCS; Scalar; WordPress; Drupal; locally developed software

Digital preservation strategy: CLOCKSS; HathiTrust; Hydra; LOCKSS; MetaArchive; Portico; in-house; digital preservation services under discussion

Additional services: marketing; outreach; training metadata dataset management; peer review management; budget preparation; author copyright advisory; other author advisory; hosting of supplemental content

ADDITIONAL INFORMATION

Plans for expansion/future directions: We are continuing to build our formal program of tiered publishing services, particularly for research journals, data, conference proceedings, and student-initiated work. PCS collaborates with the Penn State University Press, which also reports to the Dean of Libraries and Scholarly Communications. We subscribe to the principles of open access to research information and in April 2014 the University Libraries faculty voted to endorse open access publishing and submit their own scholarship to OA publishing venues whenever possible. The University Senate adopted an Open Access Resolution in April 2015.

PEPPERDINE UNIVERSITY
Pepperdine University Libraries

Primary Unit: Office of the Dean of Libraries

Primary Contact: Mark S. Roosa
Dean of Libraries
310-506-4252
mark.roosa@pepperdine.edu

PROGRAM OVERVIEW
Mission statement: The Pepperdine Libraries provide a global gateway to knowledge, serving the diverse and changing needs of our learning community through personalized service at our campus locations and rich computer-based resources. At the academic heart of our educational environment, our libraries are sanctuaries for study, learning, and research, encouraging discovery, contemplation, social discourse, and creative expression. As the information universe continues to evolve, our goal is to remain responsive to users' needs by providing seamless access to both print and digital resources essential for learning, teaching, and research. The libraries, through Pepperdine Digital Commons, offer a wide array of digital publications that are openly available for study, research, and learning.

Year publishing activities began: 2010

Organization: centralized library publishing unit/department

Total FTE in support of publishing activities: professional staff (1)

Funding sources (%): library operating budget (100)

PUBLISHING ACTIVITIES
Library publications in 2015: campus-based faculty-driven journals (1); campus-based student-driven journals (7); journals produced under contract/MOU for external groups (1); newsletters (4); ETDs (536); undergraduate capstones/honors theses (5); undergraduate student research; faculty profiles and publications; datasets

Media formats: text; images; audio; data

Disciplinary specialties: religion; business; public policy; psychology; law

Top publications: *Pepperdine Law Review* (journal); *Leaven* (journal); *Pepperdine Dispute Resolution Law Journal* (journal); *The Journal of Business, Entrepeneurship and the Law* (journal); *Journal of the National Association of Administrative Law Judiciary* (journal)

Percentage of journals that are peer reviewed: 100

Internal partners: campus departments or programs; individual faculty; graduate students; undergraduate students

External partners: Library Publishing Coalition

Publishing platform(s): bepress (Digital Commons); CONTENTdm

Digital preservation strategy: DuraCloud; LOCKSS; Portico

Additional services: marketing; outreach; training; cataloging; metadata; dataset management; digitization; audio/video streaming

ADDITIONAL INFORMATION

Plans for expansion/future directions: Publishing additional undergraduate research; creating a line of monographic publications; publishing rich media content (e.g., video presentations); implementing an enterprise digital preservation solution; identifying new ways of participating in the editorial processes generally associated with publishing.

HIGHLIGHTED PUBLICATION

The annual Seaver College Undergraduate Research and Scholarly Achievement Symposium, hosted and published by Pepperdine Digital Commons, serves to highlight and celebrate the accomplishments of student scholars.

digitalcommons.pepperdine.edu/scursas

PORTLAND STATE UNIVERSITY
Portland State University Library

Primary Unit: Digital Initiatives Unit
pdxscholar@pdx.edu

Primary Contact: Karen Bjork
Digital Initiatives Coordinator
503-725-5889
kbjork@pdx.edu

Website: pdxscholar.library.pdx.edu

PROGRAM OVERVIEW
Mission statement: Digital Initiatives and Scholarly Communication services supports new models of scholarly communications, copyright services, the showcasing of Portland State University's intellectual output via open access repository services, as well as the digitization of unique historical materials. This is achieved largely through the institutional repository PDXScholar (pdxscholar .library.pdx.edu). Major publishing initiatives include the production of the undergraduate student journals and open textbook publishing. The Library is committed to playing an active role in the changing landscape of scholarly publishing and supports the ideals of the open access movement.

Year publishing activities began: 2010

Organization: centralized library publishing unit/department

Total FTE in support of publishing activities: professional staff (2); paraprofessional staff (3.5)

Funding sources (%): library operating budget (100)

PUBLISHING ACTIVITIES
Library publications in 2015: monographs (5); technical/research reports (75); student conference papers and proceedings (27); ETDs (250); undergraduate capstones/honors theses (105)

Media formats: text; images; audio; video; data

Disciplinary specialties: urban studies and planning; environmental science; engineering and computer science; physics; education

Top publications: *Brew to Bikes: Portland's Artisan Economy* (book); *PSU McNair Scholars Online Journal* (journal); *Anthos* (journal); *Introduction to Mathematical Analysis* (textbook)

Percentage of journals that are peer reviewed: 100

Internal partners: University Honors College; McNair Scholars Program; Graduate School; Environmental Science and Management Department; College of Urban and Public Affairs; Civil and Environmental Engineering

Publishing platform(s): bepress (Digital Commons)

Digital preservation strategy: in-house

Additional services: marketing; outreach; training; analytics; cataloging; metadata; dataset management; author copyright advisory; other author advisory; digitization; image services; hosting of supplemental content

ADDITIONAL INFORMATION

Plans for expansion/future directions: Strengthen existing library publishing partnerships and expand our publishing of original research and scholarship, with a particular focus on textbook publishing and research data.

PURDUE UNIVERSITY
Purdue University Libraries

FOUNDER

Primary Unit: Purdue Scholarly Publishing Services

Primary Contact: Peter Froehlich
Head, Scholarly Publishing Services
(765) 494-8251
pfroehli@purdue.edu

Website: www.lib.purdue.edu/publishing

Social media: @PublishPurdue

PROGRAM OVERVIEW
Mission statement: To enhance the impact of Purdue scholarship by delivering high-value open information products aligned with the University's strengths; to continue to explore new models and new partnerships; to advocate for open access; and to advance the creation, communication, and discovery of new knowledge by hosting, developing, promoting, and publishing the outputs of research and of scholarly debate openly for the global community.

Year publishing activities began: 2006

Organization: centralized library publishing unit/department

Total FTE in support of publishing activities: professional staff (6.25); paraprofessional staff (1); graduate students (0.5); undergraduate students (2.5)

PUBLISHING ACTIVITIES
Library publications in 2015*: campus-based faculty-driven journals (7); campus-based student-driven journals (3); technical/research reports (118); faculty conference papers and proceedings (687); HABRI Central (an information hub for human-animal bond studies built on the HUBzero platform for scientific collaboration); the Data Curation Profiles Directory; the IMPACT Profiles Directory; the Global Policy Research Institute (GPRI) Policy Briefs

Media formats: text; images; audio; video; data; multimedia/interactive content

Disciplinary specialties: engineering (civil engineering); education (STEM); library and information science; public policy; comparative literature

*Numbers from previous years reflect journals incubated within Scholarly Publishing Services that since have been incorporated under the Purdue University Press imprint. Those journals are no longer represented here.

Top publications: Joint Transportation Research Program Technical Reports (technical reports); *JPUR: Journal of Purdue Undergraduate Research* (journal); HABRI Central (website); *CLCWeb: Comparative Literature and Culture* (journal); *Interdisciplinary Journal of Problem-based Learning* (journal)

Percentage of journals that are peer reviewed: 100

Internal partners: campus departments or programs; individual faculty; graduate students; undergraduate students

External partners: the Charleston Library Conference Board; HABRI Foundation; IATUL; the Joint Transportation Research Program

University press partners: Purdue University Press

Publishing platform(s): bepress (Digital Commons)

Digital preservation strategy: CLOCKSS; MetaArchive; Portico

Additional services: graphic design (print or web); print-on-demand; typesetting; copy-editing; marketing; outreach; training; analytics; cataloging; metadata; compiling indexes and/or TOCs; notification of A&I sources; ISSN registry; ISBN registry; DOI assignment/allocation of identifiers; open URL support; dataset management; peer review management; business model development; budget preparation; contract/license preparation; author copyright advisory; other author advisory; digitization hosting of supplemental content; audio/video streaming; developmental editing; project management

HIGHLIGHTED PUBLICATION

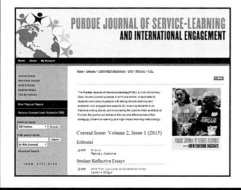

The *Purdue Journal of Service-Learning (PJSL)*, a multi-disciplinary open access journal available in print and online, is dedicated to students who conduct projects with strong service-learning and academic civic engagement aspects.

docs.lib.purdue.edu/pjsl

ADDITIONAL INFORMATION

Additional information: Purdue Scholarly Publishing Services and Purdue University Press are integrated into one unit within Purdue University Libraries and are centrally located in the heart of campus. Staff collaborate across all functions and with other colleagues in the Libraries and around Purdue. By harnessing skills of librarians and publishers, and by leveraging a common infrastructure, project teams can better adapt to changes and efficiently exploit opportunities in the digital age.

Plans for expansion/future directions: To continue to explore new opportunities, specifically in and around the digital humanities.

QUEEN'S UNIVERSITY
Queen's University Library

Primary Unit: Academic Services

Primary Contact: Rosarie Coughlan
Scholarly Publishing Librarian
613-533-6000 x77529
rosarie.coughlan@queensu.ca

Website: library.queensu.ca/scholcomm

PROGRAM OVERVIEW

Mission statement: A core strategic driver defined in the Queen's University's Strategic Framework, 2014–2019 is "research prominence." The Library's supporting strategic priority for 2014–2015 to 2016–2017 seeks to "broaden the reach of Queen's research with expanded data curation and scholarly communications services, in collaboration with and in support of emerging regional and national initiatives." Aligned to this and in support of a "balanced academy" that achieves excellence in both research as well as undergraduate and graduate education, the Library provides technology, implementation expertise, advocacy and outreach on research publication and dissemination to researchers, students, and staff seeking to disseminate their research to a global audience via open access. Current publishing activities supported by the Library include: hosting ten scholarly open access journals in partnership with Scholars Portal and the Ontario Council of University Libraries using Open Journal Systems software; hosting and disseminating Queen's University's peer-reviewed open access research through our Research Repository, QSpace including journal articles, graduate theses, conference papers, working papers, book chapters and more. The Library also provides advice and support on publication impact metrics and usage as well as guidance on other areas of open access and scholarly publishing such as open monograph publishing, open educational resources, copyright, licensing and negotiating publisher agreements.

Year publishing activities began: 2000

Organization: services are distributed across library units/departments

Total FTE in support of publishing activities: professional staff (1); paraprofessional staff (0.5)

Funding sources (%): library operating budget (100)

PUBLISHING ACTIVITIES

Library publications in 2015: campus-based faculty-driven journals (8); campus-based student-driven journals (2); faculty conference papers and proceedings (109); ETDs (548); undergraduate capstones/honors theses (77); images; datasets

Media formats: text; images; data; concept maps, modeling, maps, or other visualizations; multimedia/interactive content

Disciplinary specialties: science; history; sociology; communications; engineering

Top publications: *Surveillance and Society* (journal); The Canadian Engineering Education Association (CEEA) (conference proceedings); *Encounters in Theory and History of Education* (journal); *International Journal for Service Learning in Engineering, Humanitarian Engineering and Social Entrepreneurship* (journal); *Ideas in Ecology and Evolution* (journal)

Percentage of journals that are peer reviewed: 100

Internal partners: campus departments or programs; individual faculty; graduate students; undergraduate students

External partners: Scholars Portal; Ontario Council of University Libraries

Publishing platform(s): DSpace; OJS

Digital preservation strategy: Scholars Portal

Additional services: marketing; outreach; training; analytics; metadata; compiling indexes and/or TOCs; notification of A&I sources; ISSN registry; ISBN registry; DOI assignment/allocation of identifiers; dataset management; business model development; contract/license preparation; author copyright advisory; other author advisory

ADDITIONAL INFORMATION

Plans for expansion/future directions: We plan to integrate deposit to our institutional repository with the University's internal CV and Annual Reporting Tool (managed by University Research Services) to encourage increased deposit by Queen's faculty and researchers. We will also publish an additional two student-driven scholarly open access journals in 2015–2016.

RUTGERS UNIVERSITY
Rutgers University Libraries

Primary Unit: Technical and Automated Services

Primary Contact: Grace Agnew
Associate University Librarian for Digital Library Systems
848-445-5909
gagnew@rutgers.edu

Website: www.libraries.rutgers.edu/researchers/ru_open_access_journals

PROGRAM OVERVIEW
Mission statement: The Rutgers University Libraries support and enrich the instructional, research, and public service missions of the University through the stewardship of scholarly information and the delivery of information services. Our repository and publishing services contribute to the development of new knowledge through archiving, preserving, and publishing the results of scholarly inquiry, including ETDs, journals, and datasets.

Year publishing activities began: 2005

Organization: services are distributed across library units/departments

Total FTE in support of publishing activities: professional staff (0.5); paraprofessional staff (1.5)

Funding sources (%): library operating budget (90); grants (10)

PUBLISHING ACTIVITIES
Library publications in 2015: campus-based faculty-driven journals (4); journals produced under contract/MOU for external groups (1); technical/research reports (2); databases (4); ETDs (1040)

Media formats: text; images; audio; video; data

Disciplinary specialties: psychology; mathematics; jazz; New Jersey studies; libraries

Top publications: ETDs; *Pragmatic Case Studies in Psychotherapy* (journal); *Journal of Jazz Studies* (journal); *Journal of Rutgers University Libraries* (journal); *Electronic Journal of Boundary Elements* (journal)

Percentage of journals that are peer reviewed: 80

Internal partners: campus departments or programs; individual faculty

Publishing platform(s): Fedora; OJS

Digital preservation strategy: in-house; all issues of journals are given preservation-level archiving in our Fedora-based institutional repository in a dark archive

Additional services: graphic design (print or web); outreach; training; cataloging; metadata; ISSN registry; DOI assignment/allocation of identifiers; dataset management; contract/license preparation; author copyright advisory; digitization; image services; hosting of supplemental content; audio/video streaming

ADDITIONAL INFORMATION
Plans for expansion/future directions: Add 1–2 new journal titles per year; add datasets that are supplementary to journal articles deposited in our institutional repository; two or more additional graduate schools will participate in our ETD publishing program in the coming year.

HIGHLIGHTED PUBLICATION

Journal of Jazz Studies

The Journal of Jazz Studies is an open-access, peer-reviewed, online journal which is published by the Institute of Jazz Studies at Rutgers, The State University of New Jersey.

jjs.libraries.rutgers.edu/index.php/jjs

SEATTLE PACIFIC UNIVERSITY
Seattle Pacific University Library

Primary Unit: Scholarly Communication

Primary Contact: Kristen Hoffman
Psychology and Scholarly Communications Librarian
206-281-2423
khoffman@spu.edu

Website: digitalcommons.spu.edu

PROGRAM OVERVIEW
Mission statement: The SPU Library Scholarly Communications program, in collaboration with the Center for Scholarship and Faculty Development, exists to enhance the library's role in the discovery, creation, and sharing of faculty and student scholarship at Seattle Pacific University.

Year publishing activities began: 2014

Organization: services are distributed across campus

Total FTE in support of publishing activities: professional staff (0.5)

PUBLISHING ACTIVITIES
Library publications in 2015: faculty conference papers and proceedings (7); newsletters (2); ETDs (13); undergraduate capstones/honors theses (36); campus lectures

Media formats: text; images; audio; video; data

Disciplinary specialties: Biblical studies; educational leadership; business law, public responsibility, and ethics

Top publications: "Sects and Gender: Reaction and Resistance to Cultural Change" (conference paper); *Beyond Borders* (monograph); "Importance of School Library Programs" (white paper); "The Transformation of Persons and the Concept of Moral Order: A Study of the Evangelical Ethics of Oliver O'Donovan with Special Reference to the Barth-Brunner Debate" (thesis or dissertation); "Where Do They Go: Christian Faith and Belonging in Gay Literature" (honors project)

Internal partners: campus departments or programs; individual faculty; graduate students

Publishing platform(s): bepress (Digital Commons)

Digital preservation strategy: content is backed up through bepress (Digital Commons)

Additional services: training; author copyright advisory; hosting of supplemental content

SIMON FRASER UNIVERSITY
Simon Fraser University Library

Primary Unit: Public Knowledge Project Publishing Services (PKP/PS)
pkp-hosting@sfu.ca

Primary Contact: Brian Owen
Associate University Librarian / PKP Managing Director
778-782-7095
brian_owen@sfu.ca

Website: pkp.sfu.ca/; www.lib.sfu.ca/collections/scholarly-publishing

PROGRAM OVERVIEW
Mission statement: Provide online hosting and related technical support at no charge for scholarly journals and conferences that have a significant SFU faculty connection (e.g., Managing Editor) or to support SFU-based teaching and research initiatives.

Year publishing activities began: 2005

Organization: The SFU Library provides the administrative and technical home for PKP and its related activities, such as PKP Publishing Services. In return, PKP/PS provides the technical expertise and infrastructure support for the SFU Library's scholarly communication services. PKP/PS staff work closely with the Library's liaison librarians.

Funding sources (%): library operating budget (25); other (75)

PUBLISHING ACTIVITIES
Library publications in 2015: campus-based faculty-driven journals (9); campus-based student-driven journals (1); faculty conference papers and proceedings (2)

Media formats: text; images; audio; video; data; multimedia/interactive content

Top publications: *Canadian Journal of Communication* (journal); *International Journal of Education Policy and Leadership; Journal of Modern Hellenism* (journal); *Paideusis* (journal); *Scholarly and Research Communication* (journal)

Internal partners: SFU's Canadian Centre for Studies in Publishing

External partners: AJOL; ETCL/DHSI/INKE; IBICT; INASP; Islandora; LOCKSS; Redalyc; SciELO; SPARC

Publishing platform(s): OJS; OCS; OMP

Digital preservation strategy: COPPUL; LOCKSS

Additional services: digitization; migration from other publishing platforms; software customization/development; DOI assignment; copyright advisory

SOUTHERN ILLINOIS UNIVERSITY CARBONDALE
Morris Library

Primary Unit: OpenSIUC
opensiuc@lib.siu.edu

Primary Contact: Jonathan Nabe
Collection Development LIbrarian and Coordinator, OpenSIUC
618-453-3237
opensiuc@lib.siu.edu

Website: opensiuc.lib.siu.edu

PROGRAM OVERVIEW
Mission statement: OpenSIUC publishes online open access journals, provides access to theses, dissertations, and other select student content, and serves as one means for the preservation and open access to datasets produced by the faculty of the University.

Year publishing activities began: 2009

Organization: centralized library publishing unit/department

Total FTE in support of publishing activities: professional staff (0.25)

Funding sources (%): library operating budget (100)

PUBLISHING ACTIVITIES
Library publications in 2015: campus-based faculty-driven journals (1); campus-based student-driven journals (1); technical/research reports (4); ETDs (249); undergraduate capstones/honors theses (7); datasets

Media formats: text; images; audio; video; data

Disciplinary specialties: workforce education; communication

Top publications: *Online Journal for Workforce Education and Development* (journal)*; Kaleidoscope* (journal)

Percentage of journals that are peer reviewed: 100

Internal partners: campus departments or programs; individual faculty; graduate students; undergraduate students

University press partners: Southern Illinois University Press

Publishing platform(s): bepress (Digital Commons)

Digital preservation strategy: in implementation phase of a Private LOCKSS Network

Additional services: training; analytics; cataloging; metadata; dataset management; author copyright advisory; other author advisory; digitization hosting of supplemental content

ST. THOMAS UNIVERSITY
St. Thomas University Library

Primary Unit: St. Thomas University Library
jroach@stu.edu

Primary Contact: Dr. Jonathan Roach
Interim Dean of the Library
305-628-6627
jroach@stu.edu

Website: web.stu.edu/ThesisDissertationGuides/tabid/3719/Default.aspx

PROGRAM OVERVIEW
Mission statement: The Library engages students and faculty at their point of need and journeys with them through the research, evaluation, production, and publication processes to create new and original knowledge and learning.

Year publishing activities began: 2009

Organization: services are distributed across library units/departments

Total FTE in support of publishing activities: professional staff (0.5)

PUBLISHING ACTIVITIES
Library publications in 2015: ETDs (8)

Media formats: text

Disciplinary specialties: theology; education; humanities; social sciences; medicine

Internal partners: campus departments or programs; individual faculty; graduate students

Publishing platform(s): Proquest ETD Administrator

Digital preservation strategy: in-house

Additional services: copy-editing; outreach; training; cataloging

SUNY GENESEO
Milne Library

Primary Unit: Technical Services
publishing@geneseo.edu

Primary Contact: Kate Pitcher
Interim Director
585-245-5591
pitcher@geneseo.edu

Website: www.geneseo.edu/library/publishing

PROGRAM OVERVIEW
Mission statement: Develop a viable alternative to current commercial publishing by creating academic friendly publishing services; develop publishing expertise; and create and cultivate such expertise on campus and in other libraries for the development of emerging publishing services in libraries.

Year publishing activities began: 2011

Organization: services are distributed across library units/departments

Total FTE in support of publishing activities: professional staff (2); paraprofessional staff (1); undergraduate students (1)

Funding sources (%): endowment income (20); grants (75); sales revenue (5)

PUBLISHING ACTIVITIES
Library publications in 2015: campus-based faculty-driven journals (1); campus-based student-driven journals (1); monographs (2); textbooks (3); student conference papers and proceedings (1)

Media formats: text; images; audio; video; concept maps, modeling, maps, or other visualizations; multimedia/interactive content

Top publications: "Bob Dylan's Career as a Blakean Visionary & Romantic" (scholarly article); "Entrepreneurship in New York: The Mismatch between Venture Capital and Academic R&D" (white paper); *Tagging Along: Memories of My Grandfather James Wolcott Wadsworth, Jr.* (memoir); *The Information Literacy User's Guide: An Open, Online Textbook* (OER); *The Library Publishing Toolkit* (monograph)

Percentage of journals that are peer reviewed: 100

Internal partners: campus departments or programs; individual faculty; undergraduate students

University press partners: SUNY Press

Publishing platform(s): CONTENTdm; OJS; OMP; WordPress; locally developed software; OMEKA; Commons-in-a-box

Digital preservation strategy: in-house; digital preservation services under discussion

Additional services: graphic design (print or web); print-on-demand; typesetting; copy-editing; marketing; outreach; analytics; cataloging; metadata; ISSN registry; ISBN registry; DOI assignment/allocation of identifiers; dataset management; peer review management; business model development; contract/license preparation; author copyright advisory; other author advisory; hosting of supplemental content

ADDITIONAL INFORMATION

Plans for expansion/future directions: Currently lead a successful Open SUNY Textbooks program, which is in the process of developing a sustainability plan for ongoing operations.

SUNY PLATTSBURGH
Benjamin F. Feinberg Library

Primary Unit: Instruction and Reference Services

Primary Contact: Joshua Beatty
Senior Assistant Librarian
518-564-5200
jbeat003@plattsburgh.edu

Website: digitalcommons.plattsburgh.edu

PROGRAM OVERVIEW
Mission statement: Digital Commons @ SUNY Plattsburgh is an online collection of the intellectual output of the college including, but not limited to, works published by faculty, their research materials, and exemplary student work. The repository is intended to preserve and promote the work of the college and its academic community.

Year publishing activities began: 2012

Organization: centralized library publishing unit/department

Total FTE in support of publishing activities: librarian (0.15); undergraduates (0.125)

PUBLISHING ACTIVITIES
Library publications in 2015: campus-based faculty-driven journals (1); undergraduate capstones/honors theses (35)

Media formats: text; images; audio; video

Disciplinary specialties: expeditionary studies; college history; scholarship on teaching and learning; communication sciences and disorders; environmental science/environmental studies

Top publications: *DoNorth Magazine,* Summer/Fall 2013 (magazine); "Threading the Needles of South Dakota and Storming Devils Tower of Wyoming" (thesis or dissertation); *In Our Own Image: An Oral History of Mexican Women Filmmakers (1988–1994)* (book); "Backcountry Skiing in Alaska's White Pass" (thesis or dissertation); "Pinterest in the Writing Classroom: How Digital Curation and Collaboration Promotes Critical Thinking" (scholarly article)

Percentage of journals that are peer reviewed: 100

Internal partners: campus departments or programs; individual faculty

Publishing platform(s): bepress (Digital Commons)

Digital preservation strategy: digital preservation services under discussion

Additional services: graphic design (print or web); typesetting; marketing; outreach; training; analytics; metadata; ISSN registry; author copyright advisory; digitization; hosting of supplemental content; audio/video streaming

ADDITIONAL INFORMATION

Plans for expansion/future directions: We plan to expand on all fronts: archiving faculty and student work, digitizing Special Collections materials, and publishing more student and scholarly journals.

SYRACUSE UNIVERSITY
Syracuse University Libraries

FOUNDER

Primary Unit: Research and Scholarship

Primary Contact: Scott Warren
Interim Associate Dean for Research and Scholarship
315-443-8339
sawarr01@syr.edu

PROGRAM OVERVIEW

Mission statement: To provide Syracuse University (SU) faculty with an alternative to commercial publishing venues, and to provide the campus community support for open access publishing models.

Year publishing activities began: 2010

Organization: services are distributed across library units/departments

Total FTE in support of publishing activities: professional staff (1.5); paraprofessional staff (.5)

Funding sources (%): library operating budget (100)

PUBLISHING ACTIVITIES

Library publications in 2015: campus-based faculty-driven journals (1); campus-based student-driven journals (3); journals produced under contract/MOU for external groups (1); monographs (4); technical/research reports (270); faculty conference papers and proceedings (57); student conference papers and proceedings (15); newsletters (12); ETDs (423); undergraduate capstones/honors theses (815)

Library-administered university press publications in 2015: 50 monographs

Media formats: text; images; audio; video; concept maps, modeling, maps, or other visualizations

Disciplinary specialties: public humanities/publicly engaged scholarship; law and commerce; electrical engineering and computer science; writing and rhetoric; public diplomacy

Top publications: "Internet Adoption and Integration by Network Television News (1997 to 2004)" (thesis or dissertation); "An Efficient K-Means Clustering Algorithm" (working paper); "Data Aggregation Techniques in Sensor Networks: A Survey" (working paper); "Exploiting Data Locality in Dynamic Web Applications" (thesis or dissertation); "All the Pieces Matter: A Critical Analysis of HBO's 'The Wire'" (thesis or dissertation)

Percentage of journals that are peer reviewed: 100

Internal partners: campus departments or programs; individual faculty; graduate students; undergraduate students

External partners: Imagining America, Association of Public Diplomacy Scholars (APDS) at Syracuse University

University press partners: Syracuse University Press

Publishing platform(s): bepress (Digital Commons); CONTENTdm; OJS; WordPress; locally developed software; XTF

Digital preservation strategy: AP Trust; DPN; HathiTrust; LOCKSS; Portico; in-house; digital preservation services under discussion

Additional services: graphic design (print or web); typesetting; copy-editing; training; analytics; cataloging; metadata; notification of A&I sources; ISSN registry; ISBN registry; DOI assignment/allocation of identifiers; open URL support; peer review management; author copyright advisory; other author advisory; digitization; hosting of supplemental content; audio/video streaming

---

HIGHLIGHTED PUBLICATION

Public is a peer-reviewed, multimedia e-journal focused on humanities, arts, and design in public life. It aspires to connect what we can imagine with what we can do.

public.imaginingamerica.org/welcome

ADDITIONAL INFORMATION

Plans for expansion/future directions: Forming a new unit that will bring together several units involved in digital scholarship activities, including digital publishing; formalizing a menu of publishing services for the campus community.

TEMPLE UNIVERSITY
Temple University Libraries

Primary Unit: Digital Library Initiatives
diglib@temple.edu

Primary Contact: Delphine Khanna
Head of Digital Library Initiatives
215-204-4768
delphine@temple.edu

Website: digital.library.temple.edu

PROGRAM OVERVIEW
Mission statement: The goal of our program is to provide free and open access to digital scholarship produced by Temple University students. Currently, we focus on the publishing of doctoral dissertations, master's theses, and the winning essays of the Temple University Library Prize for Undergraduate Research in general topics and in topics related to sustainability and the environment.

Year publishing activities began: 2008

Organization: services are distributed across library units/departments

Total FTE in support of publishing activities: paraprofessional staff (0.5)

Funding sources (%): library operating budget (100)

PUBLISHING ACTIVITIES
Library publications in 2015: ETDs (292)

Media formats: text; images; audio; video; data

Disciplinary specialties: Full range of academic subjects in ETDs

Top publications: "Facebook and Other Internet Use and the Academic Performance of College Students" (thesis or dissertation); "Profitability Ratio Analysis for Professional Service Firms" (thesis or dissertation); "The Effects of Extensive Reading and Reading Strategies on Reading Self-Efficacy" (thesis or dissertation); "A Pedagogical Guide to Extended Piano Techniques" (thesis or dissertation); "Land Acquisition for Special Economic Zones in India" (thesis or dissertation)

Internal partners: campus departments or programs

Publishing platform(s): CONTENTdm; OJS

Digital preservation strategy: in-house; digital preservation services under discussion; HathiTrust; backup of CONTENTdm instance via OCLC

Additional services: cataloging; metadata; DOI assignment/allocation of identifiers; digitization; hosting of supplemental content

ADDITIONAL INFORMATION
Plans for expansion/future directions: Now that Temple Libraries has a new Scholarly Communication Officer, there will be expanded publication offerings. Pilot digital preservation projects in Hydra are being developed for the future.

TULANE UNIVERSITY
Howard-Tilton Memorial Library

Primary Unit: Digital Initiatives & Publishing

Primary Contact: Jeff Rubin
Digital Initiatives and Publishing Coordinator
504-247-1832
jrubin6@tulane.edu

Website: library.tulane.edu/repository

PROGRAM OVERVIEW
Mission statement: Tulane University Journal Publishing is an open access journal publishing service that provides a web-based platform for scholarly and academic publishing to the Tulane community.

Year publishing activities began: 2012

Organization: centralized library publishing unit/department

Total FTE in support of publishing activities: professional staff (1)

Funding sources (%): library operating budget (100)

PUBLISHING ACTIVITIES
Library publications in 2015: campus-based faculty-driven journals (1); campus-based student-driven journals (1); ETDs (145); non-peer reviewed academic and non-academic papers; reports; magazines

Media formats: text; images; audio; video

Disciplinary specialties: gender studies, law, public health

Top publications: *Tulane Undergraduate Research Journal* (journal); *Newcomb College Institute Research on Women, Gender, & Feminism* (journal); *The Journal of Community Health Promotion and Research* (journal); *Tulane Studies in Zoology and Botany* (journal); *Tulane Journal of International Affairs* (journal)

Percentage of journals that are peer reviewed: 100

Internal partners: campus departments or programs; individual faculty; graduate students; undergraduate students

Publishing platform(s): Islandora; OJS

Digital preservation strategy: DPN; digital preservation services under discussion

Additional services: training; metadata; ISSN registry; author copyright advisory; hosting of supplemental content; audio/video streaming

ADDITIONAL INFORMATION

Plans for expansion/future directions: Tulane University Journal Publishing now offers an additional tier of publishing services for non-peer reviewed academic and university content.

UNIVERSITÉ LAVAL
Bibliothèque

Primary Unit: Direction du soutien à la recherche et à l'apprentissage (DSRA)

Primary Contact: Pierre Lasou
Scholarly Communication Librarian
418-656-2131 x12522
pierre.lasou@bibl.ulaval.ca

PROGRAM OVERVIEW
Mission statement: The library ETD program disseminates theses and dissertations submitted to Université Laval Faculty of Graduate Studies.

Year publishing activities began: 2002

Organization: centralized library publishing unit/department

Total FTE in support of publishing activities: professional staff (2)

Funding sources (%): library operating budget (100)

PUBLISHING ACTIVITIES
Library publications in 2015: ETDs (800)

Media formats: text; images; audio; video

Internal partners: campus departments or programs

Publishing platform(s): locally developed software

Digital preservation strategy: digital preservation services under discussion

ADDITIONAL INFORMATION
Plans for expansion/future directions: In the short run, Library publishing services will be expanded by our institutional repository.

UNIVERSITY OF ALBERTA
University of Alberta Libraries

Primary Unit: Digital Initiatives

Primary Contact: Sonya Betz (until March 2016)
Acting Digital Repository Services Librarian
780-492-1718
sonya.betz@ualberta.ca

PROGRAM OVERVIEW
Mission statement: The University of Alberta Libraries extends hosting and publishing support to members of the University of Alberta community who wish to publish in OA formats.

Year publishing activities began: 2007

Organization: centralized library publishing unit/department

Total FTE in support of publishing activities: professional staff (1); paraprofessional staff (0.3); graduate students (0.2)

Funding sources (%): library operating budget (100)

PUBLISHING ACTIVITIES
Library publications in 2015: campus-based faculty-driven journals (23); campus-based student-driven journals (8); journals produced under contract/ MOU for external groups (1)

Media formats: text; images; audio; video; data; concept maps, modeling, maps, or other visualizations; multimedia/interactive content

Disciplinary specialties: library and information studies; education; sociology; pharmaceutical sciences; environmental studies

Top publications: *Canadian Journal of Sociology* (journal); *International Journal of Qualitative Methods* (journal); *Journal of Pharmacy & Pharmaceutical Sciences* (journal); *Evidence Based Library and Information Practice* (journal); *Canadian Review of Comparative Literature* (journal)

Percentage of journals that are peer reviewed: 75

Internal partners: campus departments or programs; individual faculty; graduate students; undergraduate students

121

External partners: Public Knowledge Project; research teams/projects (e.g., Oil Sands Research and Information Network); local non-profit organizations (e.g., Edmonton Social Planning Council)

Publishing platform(s): Fedora; OJS; locally developed software; Dataverse; Hydra

Digital preservation strategy: Archive-It; Archivematica; CLOCKSS; COPPUL; HathiTrust; LOCKSS; Portico; Hydra; in-house

Additional services: training; notification of A&I sources; DOI assignment/allocation of identifiers; dataset management; hosting of supplemental content

ADDITIONAL INFORMATION

Plans for expansion/future directions: We are advancing data publishing services via a Dataverse instance we plan to connect to OJS; we are implementing DOI registration and CrossRef to EZID; migrating IR and digital collections to Hydra DAMS.

UNIVERSITY OF ARIZONA
University of Arizona Libraries

Primary Unit: Office of Digital Innovation and Stewardship

Primary Contact: Dan Lee
Director, Office of Copyright Management & Scholarly Communication
520-621-6433
leed@email.arizona.edu

PROGRAM OVERVIEW

Mission statement: The Office of Digital Innovation and Stewardship provides tools, services, and expertise that enable the creation, distribution, and preservation of scholarly works and research data in support of the mission of the University of Arizona.

Year publishing activities began: 1994

Organization: centralized library publishing unit/department

Total FTE in support of publishing activities: professional staff (3.25); paraprofessional staff (1); graduate students (0.5)

Funding sources (%): library operating budget (100)

PUBLISHING ACTIVITIES

Library publications in 2015: campus-based faculty-driven journals (5); campus-based student-driven journals (2); journals produced under contract/ MOU for external groups (1); faculty conference papers and proceedings (25); student conference papers and proceedings (50); newsletters (2); ETDs (6,563); undergraduate capstones/honors theses (62)

Media formats: text; images; audio; video; data

Disciplinary specialties: agriculture; life sciences; dendrochronology; archaeology; geosciences

Top publications: *Radiocarbon* (journal); *Journal of Ancient Egyptian Interconnections* (journal); *Lymphology* (journal); *Arizona Anthropologist* (journal); ETDs

Percentage of journals that are peer reviewed: 100

Internal partners: campus departments or programs; individual faculty; graduate students; undergraduate students

External partners: International Society of Lymphology; Society for Range Management; Tree Ring Society; Arizona-Nevada Academy of Science

University press partners: University of Arizona Press

Publishing platform(s): CONTENTdm; DSpace; OJS; locally developed software

Digital preservation strategy: Amazon S3; LOCKSS; in-house

Additional services: print-on-demand training; analytics; cataloging; metadata; ISSN registry; ISBN registry; author copyright advisory; other author advisory; digitization; hosting of supplemental content

ADDITIONAL INFORMATION

Plans for expansion/future directions: Discussing collaborative efforts with the university press.

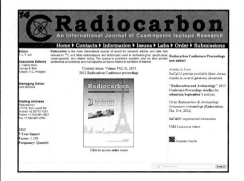

HIGHLIGHTED PUBLICATION

Radiocarbon is the main international journal of record for research articles and date lists relevant to 14C and other radioisotopes and techniques used in archaeological, geophysical, oceanographic, and related dating.

www.radiocarbon.org

UNIVERSITY OF BRITISH COLUMBIA
University of British Columbia Library

Primary Unit: Digital Initiatives

Primary Contact: Bronwen Sprout
Head, Digital Programs and Services
604-827-3953
bronwen.sprout@ubc.ca

Website: digitize.library.ubc.ca; circle.ubc.ca

Social media: @cIRcle_UBC; @DigitizeUBC

PROGRAM OVERVIEW
Mission statement: Digital Initiatives is a key part of the Library's strategy to support the evolving needs of faculty and students and to support teaching, research, and learning at UBC. Our goal is to create sustainable, world-class programs and processes that promote digital scholarship, make UBC research and digital collections openly available to the world, and ensure the long-term preservation of UBC's digital collections. cIRcle is an open access digital repository for published and unpublished material created by the UBC community and its partners. Its aim is to showcase and preserve UBC's unique intellectual output by making content freely available to anyone, anywhere via the web.

Year publishing activities began: 2007

Organization: services are distributed across library units/departments

Total FTE in support of publishing activities: professional staff (2); paraprofessional staff (1)

Funding sources (%): library operating budget (100)

PUBLISHING ACTIVITIES
Library publications in 2015: campus-based faculty-driven journals (8); campus-based student-driven journals (10); faculty conference papers and proceedings (683); student conference papers and proceedings (1); ETDs (1,587); undergraduate capstones/honors theses (78)

Media formats: text; images; audio; video; data

Disciplinary specialties: mining engineering; mathematics; forestry; education; earth and ocean sciences

Top publications: BIRS Workshop Lecture Videos (video series); *Guidelines for Mine Haul Road Design* (book)

Percentage of journals that are peer reviewed: 75

Internal partners: individual faculty; graduate students; undergraduate students

External partners: Banff International Research Station for Mathematical Innovation and Discovery (BIRS); emerita

University press partners: UBC Press

Publishing platform(s): CONTENTdm; DSpace; OJS; WordPress

Digital preservation strategy: Archive-It; Archivematica; CLOCKSS; COPPUL

Additional services: cataloging; metadata; author copyright advisory; digitization hosting of supplemental content; audio/video streaming; analytics

UNIVERSITY OF CALIFORNIA
California Digital Library

Primary Unit: California Digital Library
help@escholarship.org

Primary Contact: Catherine Mitchell
Director, Access & Publishing; Operations Director, Office of Scholarly
Communication
510-587-6132
catherine.mitchell@ucop.edu

Website: www.escholarship.org

Social media: facebook.com/eScholarship; @eScholarship

PROGRAM OVERVIEW

Mission statement: The CDL Publishing team provides open access digital
publication services to the University of California academic community,
supports widespread distribution of UC research materials, and fosters new
models of scholarly publishing through the development and application of
advanced technologies. The CDL's suite of publication services includes a system-
wide digital publications platform as well as tools to support the UC Open
Access Policy. All of these services are a part of UC's broader effort to ensure a
sustainable scholarly publishing system in the service of the University's research
and teaching enterprise.

Year publishing activities began: 2002

Organization: At the CDL, the publishing activities are centered in the Access
& Publishing group. However, other publishing activities occur across the UC
system, some of which use eScholarship, but not all.

Total FTE in support of publishing activities: professional staff (6)

Funding sources (%): library operating budget (100)

PUBLISHING ACTIVITIES

Library publications in 2015: campus-based faculty-driven journals (43);
campus-based student-driven journals (32); monographs (201); technical/
research reports (23,969); faculty conference papers and proceedings (154);
student conference papers and proceedings (96); ETDs (13,531); undergraduate
capstones/honors theses (176)

Media formats: text; images; audio; video; data; concept maps, modeling, maps, or other visualizations; we display PDF (rendered as an image), but can accept any format of file as a supplemental file and allow end users to download it.

Disciplinary specialties: eScholarship has no particular domain focus. We support the entire range of academic inquiry, from established disciplines to newly emerging fields.

Top publications: *Assessing the Future Landscape of Scholarly Communication: An Exploration of Faculty Values and Needs in Seven Disciplines* (book); California Classical Studies (book series); *Western Journal of Emergency Medicine* (journal); *California Agriculture* (journal); *Dermatology Online Journal* (journal)

Percentage of journals that are peer reviewed: 100

Internal partners: campus departments or programs; individual faculty; graduate students; undergraduate students

External partners: UC Press

Publishing platform(s): OJS; locally developed software; XTF

Digital preservation strategy: UC3 Merritt

Additional services: print-on-demand training; analytics; notification of A&I sources; ISSN registry; DOI assignment/allocation of identifiers; open URL support; author copyright advisory; hosting of supplemental content; audio/video streaming

ADDITIONAL INFORMATION

Additional information: eScholarship is also the repository for UC faculty postprints, of which we currently have 31,225.

Plans for expansion/future directions: We are currently integrating the eScholarship publishing platform with a publication harvesting system from Symplectic Elements, in order to support UC faculty in their efforts to comply with their Open Access Policy. Harvested and claimed items will have an authorized article made available in eScholarship. In addition, we are exploring new strategies for digital-first monograph publishing and are conducting research with UC-based digital humanists to get a better understanding of their research and publishing needs and how we might support them.

UNIVERSITY OF CHICAGO
University of Chicago Library

Primary Unit: Digital Services

Primary Contact: Amy Buckland
Institutional Repository Manager
773-834-7377
amybuckland@uchicago.edu

PROGRAM OVERVIEW
Year publishing activities began: 2015

Organization: centralized library publishing unit/department

Total FTE in support of publishing activities: professional staff (0.3); paraprofessional staff (0.1)

Funding sources (%): library operating budget (100)

PUBLISHING ACTIVITIES
Internal partners: campus departments or programs; individual faculty; graduate students; undergraduate students

Publishing platform(s): bepress (Digital Commons); DSpace; locally developed software

Digital preservation strategy: AP Trust; HathiTrust; in-house

Additional services: outreach; training; DOI assignment/allocation of identifiers; dataset management; author copyright advisory; other author advisory; hosting of supplemental content

ADDITIONAL INFORMATION
Plans for expansion/future directions: The library plans to begin a journal publishing program.

UNIVERSITY OF FLORIDA
George A. Smathers Libraries

Primary Unit: Digital Production Services
ufdc@uflib.ufl.edu

Primary Contact: Judith C. Russell
Dean of University Libraries
352-273-2505
jcrussell@ufl.edu

Website: ufdc.ufl.edu; www.digital.uflib.ufl.edu

PROGRAM OVERVIEW
Mission statement: The Digital Production Services unit develops, manages, and publishes digital content from curatorial collections, in support of academic programs, organizes conversion and ingest capabilities, facilitates awareness, and coordinates instruction in scholarly use and development of digital technologies and their application to collection and publishing services.

Organization: services are distributed across library units/departments

Funding sources (%): library operating budget (100)

PUBLISHING ACTIVITIES
Library publications in 2015: campus-based faculty-driven journals (8); campus-based student-driven journals (3); journals produced under contract/MOU for external groups (1); newsletters (1); databases (14); ETDs (1,174); undergraduate capstones/honors theses (43); undergraduate non-honors theses (3)

Media formats: text; images; audio; video; data; concept maps, modeling, maps, or other visualizations

Disciplinary specialties: Carribean studies; African studies; entomology; psychology; physical therapy

Top publications: ARL Position Description Bank; *African Studies Quarterly* (journal); *Interamerican Journal of Psychology* (journal); *Journal of Undergraduate Research* (journal); *Chemical Engineering Education* (journal)

Percentage of journals that are peer reviewed: 100

Internal partners: campus departments or programs; individual faculty; graduate students; undergraduate students

External partners: Florida Anthropological Society; Florida Horticultural Society; Florida Geological Survey; Medical Anthropology Quarterly (post-print archive); Florida Entomological Society; St. Augustine Historical Society; Panama Canal Society; Rossica Society of Russian Philately; Florida Digital Newspaper Library; Caribbean Newspaper Digital Library

University press partners: University Press of Florida; University of Florida Press

Publishing platform(s): OJS; locally developed software; Scalar; SobekCM; WordPress

Digital preservation strategy: DPN; FCLA DAITSS; HathiTrust; in-house

Additional services: marketing; outreach; training; analytics; cataloging; metadata; TOCs; notification of A&I sources; ISSN registry; ISBN registry; DOI assignment/allocation of identifiers; open URL support; dataset management; business model development; author copyright advisory; other author advisory; digitization; image services; data visualization; hosting of supplemental content; audio/video streaming; other

ADDITIONAL INFORMATION

Plans for expansion/future directions: New activities and future plans include the print publishing of limited editions of artists books, reprinting out-of-print books for which the libraries own the rights, and publishing of limited edition and print-on-demand books related to the history of the university and library special collections, as well as additional support for the publishing of innovative digital scholarship. Future plans include close collaboration with the University Press for new publishing initiatives and coordinated complementary publishing activities through the LibraryPress@UF.

UNIVERSITY OF GUELPH
University of Guelph Library

Primary Unit: Research Enterprise and Scholarly Communication
lib.research@uoguelph.ca

Primary Contact: Wayne Johnston
Head, Research Enterprise and Scholarly Communication
519-824-4120 x56900
wajohnst@uoguelph.ca

Website: www.lib.uoguelph.ca/get-assistance/publishing-support

PROGRAM OVERVIEW
Mission statement: The Library maintains an Open Journal System, a platform which maintains, stores, and automates the publishing process for online, open access journals. The University of Guelph Library currently hosts 17 open access journals through our Open Journal System.

Year publishing activities began: 2004

Organization: centralized library publishing unit/department

Total FTE in support of publishing activities: professional staff (60)

Funding sources (%): library operating budget (100)

PUBLISHING ACTIVITIES
Library publications in 2015: campus-based faculty-driven journals (4); campus-based student-driven journals (5); journals produced under contract/MOU for external groups (5); databases (24); ETDs (550)

Media formats: text; images; audio; video; data

Disciplinary specialties: improvisational music; French language and culture; Scottish history; African education; library science

Top publications: *Critical Studies in Improvisation* (journal); *International Review of Scottish Studies* (journal); *Nouvelle Revue Synergies Canada* (journal); *African Journal of Teacher Education* (journal); *Partnership: the Canadian Journal of Library and Information Practice and Research* (journal)

Percentage of journals that are peer reviewed: 90

Internal partners: campus departments or programs; individual faculty; graduate students; undergraduate students

Publishing platform(s): DSpace; Fedora; OJS

Digital preservation strategy: Scholars Portal

Additional services: graphic design (print or web); training; analytics; dataset management; author copyright advisory; other author advisory; audio/video streaming

UNIVERSITY OF HAWAII AT MANOA
University of Hawaii at Manoa Library

Primary Unit: Desktop Network Services

Primary Contact: Beth Tillinghast
Interim Assistant University Librarian for Information Technology
808-956-2742
betht@hawaii.edu

PROGRAM OVERVIEW
Mission statement: Though the University of Hawaii at Manoa currently does not have a formal library publishing program, our library is involved in providing publishing services through the various collections hosted in our institutional repository, ScholarSpace. We provide the hosting services for numerous department journal publications, conference proceedings, technical reports, department newsletters, as well as open access to some dissertations and theses. The publishing activities are consistent with our mission of acquiring, organizing, preserving, and providing access to information resources vital to the learning, teaching, and research mission of the University of Hawaii at Manoa.

Year publishing activities began: 2007

Organization: services are distributed across campus

Total FTE in support of publishing activities: professional staff (0.1); paraprofessional staff (0.1); graduate students (0.2)

Funding sources (%): library operating budget (85); non-library campus budget (10); charge backs (5)

PUBLISHING ACTIVITIES
Library publications in 2015: campus-based faculty-driven journals (5); campus-based student-driven journals (1); technical/research reports (20); faculty conference papers and proceedings (6); newsletters (12); databases (5); ETDs (50)

Media formats: text; images; audio; video; data; multimedia/interactive content

Disciplinary specialties: language documentation; social work; entomology; Pacific Islands culture; Southeast Asian culture

Top publications: *Ethnobotany Research and Applications* (journal); *Language Documentation and Conservation* (journal); *The Contemporary Pacific* (journal); *Journal of Indigenous Social Development* (journal); *Explorations* (journal)

Percentage of journals that are peer reviewed: 100

Internal partners: campus departments or programs

Publishing platform(s): DSpace

Digital preservation strategy: Archive-It; Portico; in-house; digital preservation services under discussion

Additional services: metadata; DOI assignment/allocation of identifiers; digitization

ADDITIONAL INFORMATION

Plans for expansion/future directions: We are working with our University Press to explore ways of collaboration as well as with the Outreach College in support of publishing Open Educational Resources.

UNIVERSITY OF ILLINOIS AT CHICAGO
University Library

Primary Unit: Scholarly Communications
escholarship@uic.edu

Primary Contact: Sandy De Groote
Scholarly Communication Librarian
312-413-9494
sgroote@uic.edu

Website: library.uic.edu/home/services/escholarship

PROGRAM OVERVIEW
Mission statement: The objective/mission of the UIC University Library publishing program is to advance scholarly knowledge in a cost-effective manner.

Year publishing activities began: 2007

Organization: centralized library publishing unit/department

Total FTE in support of publishing activities: professional staff (1); undergraduate students (3)

Funding sources (%): library operating budget (70); charge backs (30)

PUBLISHING ACTIVITIES
Library publications in 2015: campus-based faculty-driven journals (5); campus-based student-driven journals (2); technical/research reports (2); newsletters (1); ETDs (700)

Media formats: text; images; data

Disciplinary specialties: social work; Internet studies; public health informatics

Top publications: *First Monday* (journal); *Online Journal of Public Health Informatics* (journal); *Behavior and Social Issues* (journal); *Uncommon Culture* (journal); *Journal of Biomedical Discovery and Collaboration* (journal)

Percentage of journals that are peer reviewed: 80

Internal partners: campus departments or programs; individual faculty

Publishing platform(s): DSpace; OJS

Digital preservation strategy: LOCKSS

Additional services: typesetting; cataloging; metadata; notification of A&I sources; DOI assignment/allocation of identifiers

ADDITIONAL INFORMATION
Plans for expansion/future directions: Publish additional journals, publish data.

UNIVERSITY OF ILLINOIS URBANA-CHAMPAIGN
University Library

Primary Unit: Scholarly Communications and Publishing Unit

Primary Contact: Aaron McCollough
Head, Scholarly Communications and Publishing
217-265-5390
amccollo@illinois.edu

Website: www.library.illinois.edu/sc/services/scholarly_communications/index.html

PROGRAM OVERVIEW

Mission statement: The University of Illinois Scholarly Communications and Publishing Unit is an essential part of the library's long-standing efforts in offering scholarly preservation, dissemination, and access solutions to faculty and students at the University and beyond. In partnership with other campus units, including the Office of Undergraduate Research, the Illinois Program for Research in the Humanities, the University of Illinois Press, and others, the unit is currently in the process of developing high-quality scholarly publishing venues in addition to its suite of scholarly communications training and consulting services. We were established to help student and faculty researchers navigate all of the key functions of the publishing process. We are responsible for rights, permissions, and contracts consultations, institutional repository management, as well as journal, book, and multimodal scholarly publication development and support.

Year publishing activities began: 2010

Organization: centralized library publishing unit/department

Total FTE in support of publishing activities: professional staff (4.5)

Funding sources (%): library operating budget (66); non-library campus budget (2); endowment income (22); grants (10)

PUBLISHING ACTIVITIES

Library publications in 2015: campus-based student-driven journals (5); ETDs (2,200); exhibition catalogs

Media formats: text; images; audio; video

Disciplinary specialties: literary criticism; ethnography; agriculture, consumer, and environmental sciences; social work

Percentage of journals that are peer reviewed: 80

Internal partners: campus departments or programs; individual faculty; graduate students; undergraduate students

University press partners: University of Illinois Press; University of Michigan Press; University of Minnesota Press

Publishing platform(s): CONTENTdm; DSpace; OJS

Digital preservation strategy: in-house

Additional services: outreach; training; cataloging; metadata; ISSN registry; peer review management; author copyright advisory; digitization

ADDITIONAL INFORMATION
Plans for expansion/future directions: Journal, monographic, and "digital scholarship" publishing activities (as well as consultation around all three of these) scaling up in the coming 12 months.

UNIVERSITY OF IOWA
University of Iowa Libraries

Primary Unit: Digital Scholarship & Publishing Studio

Primary Contact: Wendy Robertson
Digital Scholarship Librarian
319-335-5821
wendy-robertson@uiowa.edu

Website: lib.uiowa.edu/drp/publishing

Social media: @IowaResO

PROGRAM OVERVIEW

Mission statement: The department explores ways that academic libraries can best leverage digital collections, resources, and expertise to support faculty and student scholars by collaborating on interdisciplinary scholarship built upon digital collection, offering publishing services to support sustainable scholarly communication, engaging the community through participatory digital initiatives, promoting widespread use and reuse of locally built repositories and archives, and advancing new technologies that support digital research and publishing.

Year publishing activities began: 2009

Organization: centralized library publishing unit/department

Total FTE in support of publishing activities: professional staff (0.6)

Funding sources (%): library materials budget (100)

PUBLISHING ACTIVITIES

Library publications in 2015: campus-based faculty-driven journals (8); campus-based student-driven journals (3); journals produced under contract/MOU for external groups (2); technical/research reports (18); faculty conference papers and proceedings (203); newsletters (11); ETDs (560)

Media formats: text; audio, video; data

Top publications: *Walt Whitman Quarterly Review* (journal); *Annals of Iowa* (journal); *Medieval Feminist Forum* (journal); *Iowa Journal of Cultural Studies* (journal); *Poroi* (journal)

Percentage of journals that are peer reviewed: 77

Internal partners: campus departments or programs; individual faculty; graduate students

External partners: Society for Medieval Feminist Scholarship; State Historical Society of Iowa

Publishing platform(s): bepress (Digital Commons); CONTENTdm; WordPress; locally developed software

Digital preservation strategy: Archive-It; LOCKSS; Portico; in-house

Additional services: graphic design (print or web) copy-editing training; analytics; cataloging; metadata; notification of A&I sources; ISSN registry; DOI assignment/allocation of identifiers; open URL support; dataset management; peer review management; digitization; hosting of supplemental content; audio/video streaming

ADDITIONAL INFORMATION
Additional information: In addition to the publication types listed, we will publish other content for faculty, including supplemental content to published items, and sometimes work on extensive projects with them. This is extremely variable by year.

UNIVERSITY OF KANSAS
KU Libraries

Primary Unit: Center for Faculty Initiatives & Engagement and IT & Discovery Services
lib_cfie@ku.edu

Primary Contact: Marianne Reed
Digital Initiatives Coordinator
785-864-8913
mreed@ku.edu

Website: journals.ku.edu

PROGRAM OVERVIEW
Mission statement: Digital Publishing Services provides support to the KU community for the design, management, and distribution of online publications, including journals, conference proceedings, monographs, and other scholarly content. We help scholars explore new and emerging publishing models in our changing scholarly communication environment, and we help monitor and address campus concerns and questions about electronic publishing. These services are intended to enable online publishing for campus publications, and help make their content available in a manner that promotes increased visibility and access, and ensures long-term stewardship of the materials.

Year publishing activities began: 2007

Organization: Combination of centralized library publishing unit/department and some other support services distributed across library units/departments (like IT support)

Total FTE in support of publishing activities: professional staff (0.3)

Funding sources (%): library operating budget (100)

PUBLISHING ACTIVITIES
Library publications in 2015: campus-based faculty-driven journals (18); campus-based student-driven journals (2); ETDs (479); undergraduate capstones/honors theses (6); department-sponsored lectures (1); oral histories and interviews (199); radio spots produced by departments (312); departmental publication series (88)

Media formats: text; images; audio; video; data

Disciplinary specialties: theater and film; American studies; sociology; Slavic languages and literatures; ecology and evolutionary biology

Top publications: *Latin American Theatre Review* (journal); *American Studies* (journal); *Journal of Dramatic Theory and Criticism* (journal); *Social Thought and Research* (journal); *Auslegung: A Journal of Philosophy* (journal)

Percentage of journals that are peer reviewed: 100

Internal partners: campus departments or programs; individual faculty; graduate students

External partners: Mid-America American Studies Association; Slavic and East European Folklore Association; American Montessori Society

University press partners: University Press of Kansas

Publishing platform(s): DSpace; OJS

Digital preservation strategy: Portico; digital preservation services under discussion

Additional services: outreach; training; analytics; cataloging; metadata; ISBN registry; DOIs assignment/allocation of identifiers; author copyright advisory; digitization; hosting of supplemental content; audio/video streaming; consulting on publishing models and issues

ADDITIONAL INFORMATION
Additional information: The Library produces the Resources for Editors of Scholarly Journals LibGuide: guides.lib.ku.edu/journal_editors.

Plans for expansion/future directions: Some services are ongoing. A strategic initiative to expand the program is pending.

UNIVERSITY OF KENTUCKY
University of Kentucky Libraries

Primary Unit: Digital Scholarship
UKnowledge@lsv.uky.edu

Primary Contact: Adrian K. Ho
Director of Digital Scholarship
859-218-0895
adrian.ho@uky.edu

Website: uknowledge.uky.edu

PROGRAM OVERVIEW
Mission statement: The University of Kentucky (UK) Libraries launched an institutional repository (UKnowledge: uknowledge.uky.edu) in late 2010 to champion the integration and transformation of scholarly communication within the UK community. The initiative sought to improve students', faculty members', and researchers' access to appropriate resources for maximizing the dissemination of their research and scholarship in an open and digital environment. A crucial component of UKnowledge is providing publishing services to broadly disseminate scholarship created or sponsored by the UK community. We provide a flexible platform to publish a variety of scholarly content and to expand the discoverability of the published works. Using state-of-the-art technologies, we are able to offer campus constituents sought-after services in different stages of the scholarly communication lifecycle to help them thrive and succeed. We also inform them of scholarly communication issues such as open access, author rights, open licensing, altmetrics, researcher identity management, and the economics of scholarly publishing. Providing library publishing services is one avenue through which we are making significant contributions to the fulfillment of UK's mission.

Year publishing activities began: 2010

Organization: services are distributed across library units/departments

Total FTE in support of publishing activities: professional staff (1); paraprofessional staff (1); student assistant (0.5)

Funding sources (%): library materials budget (100)

PUBLISHING ACTIVITIES
Library publications in 2015: campus-based faculty-driven journals (3); campus-based student-driven journals (2); technical/research reports (75); faculty conference papers and proceedings (6); newsletters (4); ETDs (468); undergraduate capstones/honors theses (4); graduate capstone projects (281); image galleries (20)

Media formats: text; images; video

Disciplinary specialties: cardiology; higher education; Hispanic studies; public health; social theory

Top publications: *Kentucky Journal of Higher Education Policy and Practice* (journal); *Nomenclatura: Aproximaciones a los estudios hispánicos* (journal); *Frontiers in Public Health Services and Systems Research* (journal); *disClosure: A Journal of Social Theory* (journal); *The VAD Journal: Journal of Mechanical Assisted Circulation and Heart Failure* (journal)

Percentage of journals that are peer reviewed: 100

Internal partners: campus departments or programs; individual faculty; graduate students

University press partners: University Press of Kentucky

Publishing platform(s): bepress (Digital Commons)

Digital preservation strategy: digital preservation services under discussion

Additional services: graphic design (print or web); marketing; training; analytics; cataloging; metadata; notification of A&I sources; ISSN registry; open URL support; peer review management contract/license preparation; author copyright advisory; other author advisory; digitization hosting of supplemental content; DOI assignment

ADDITIONAL INFORMATION
Additional information: One thousand and thirty-five monographs published by the University Press of Kentucky are freely available to the faculty, students, and staff of the University of Kentucky via UKnowledge.

Plans for expansion/future directions: UK Libraries will continue to strengthen existing library publishing partnerships, bring more campus constituents on board, and build upon our current library publishing services. We will pursue additional opportunities to collaborate with various campus units in support of undergraduate research as we celebrate UK students' academic achievements by making them visible and accessible worldwide. We also will assist UK-based print journals to create their online presence and extend their reach beyond academia. Through partnerships with UK researchers, we will explore data publishing. Last but not least, we will continue to advocate open access and open licensing, as well as inform the UK community of new scholarly communication practices, such as alternative metrics, open peer review, and researcher identity management. We look forward to UKnowledge being the primary online publishing avenue for UK-based research and scholarship.

UNIVERSITY OF MARYLAND
University of Maryland Libraries

Primary Unit: Digital Programs and Initiatives

Primary Contact: Terry M. Owen
Digital Scholarship Librarian
301-314-1328
towen@umd.edu

Website: publish.lib.umd.edu; drum.lib.umd.edu

PROGRAM OVERVIEW
Mission statement: Capture, preserve, and provide access to the output of the University of Maryland faculty, researchers, centers, and labs, and provide new modes of scholarly publishing.

Year publishing activities began: 2004

Organization: centralized library publishing unit/department

Total FTE in support of publishing activities: professional staff (1); graduate students (0.5)

Funding sources (%): library operating budget (100)

PUBLISHING ACTIVITIES
Library publications in 2015: campus-based faculty-driven journals (1); campus-based student-driven journals (1); technical/research reports (14); newsletters (2); ETDs (956); undergraduate capstones/honors theses (11); specialized digital projects (2)

Media formats: text; images; audio; video; data

Percentage of journals that are peer reviewed: 50

Internal partners: campus departments or programs; individual faculty; graduate students; undergraduate students

Publishing platform(s): DSpace; Fedora; OJS; WordPress, Omeka

Digital preservation strategy: in-house; digital preservation services under discussion

Additional services: marketing; outreach; training; analytics; cataloging; metadata; notification of A&I sources; ISSN registry; DOI assignment/allocation of identifiers; open URL support; dataset management; peer review management; author copyright advisory; hosting of supplemental content; audio/video streaming

UNIVERSITY OF MASSACHUSETTS AMHERST

University of Massachusetts Amherst Libraries

Primary Unit: Office of Scholarly Communication
scholarworks@library.umass.edu

Primary Contact: Marilyn S. Billings
Scholarly Communication & Special Initiatives Librarian
413-545-6891
mbillings@library.umass.edu

Website: scholarworks.umass.edu/; library.umass.edu/scholarly-communication

Social media: @ScholCommUMA

PROGRAM OVERVIEW

Mission statement: ScholarWorks@UMass Amherst is a digital repository for the research and scholarly output of members of the University of Massachusetts Amherst community, administered by the UMass Amherst Libraries. It is a way for UMass Amherst scholars to organize, store, and preserve research in a single unified location. It can accommodate virtually any publication, presentation, or production in electronic format, including journal articles, conference materials, books, theses and dissertations, educational materials, datasets, working papers, and image, video, and audio files. These services enhance the professional visibility for faculty and researchers, and provide excellent search and retrieval facilities and broader dissemination.

Year publishing activities began: 2006

Organization: centralized library publishing unit/department

Total FTE in support of publishing activities: professional staff (4); paraprofessional staff (1); undergraduates (3)

Funding sources (%): library materials budget (30); library operating budget (70)

PUBLISHING ACTIVITIES

Library publications in 2015: campus-based faculty-driven journals (5); campus-based student-driven journals (2); monographs (6); textbooks (3); technical/research reports (1000); faculty conference papers and proceedings (4); newsletters (2); databases (1); ETDs (4000)

Media formats: text; images; video; data; tables and graphs; maps; embedded streaming media

Disciplinary specialties: anthropology; communication; cultural studies; botany; statistics

Top publications: *How to Do Case Study Research* (monograph); *Landscapes of Violence* (journal); *communication +1* (journal); *Journal of Medicinally Active Plants* (journal)

Percentage of journals that are peer reviewed: 75

Internal partners: campus departments or programs; individual faculty; graduate students; undergraduate students

External partners: American Council for Medicinally Active Plants; International Dose-Response Society; Northeastern Recreation Research Symposium; Tourism Travel and Research Association; USBI Biochar

University press partners: University of Massachusetts Amherst

Publishing platform(s): bepress (Digital Commons); Eprints, Fedora

Digital preservation strategy: CLOCKSS; LOCKSS

HIGHLIGHTED PUBLICATION

communication +1 provides an open forum for exploring and sharing ideas about communication across modes of inquiry and perspectives. Its primary objective is to push the theoretical frontiers of communication as an autonomous and distinct field of research.

scholarworks.umass.edu/cpo

Additional services: print-on-demand; marketing; outreach; training; analytics; metadata; ISSN registry; open URL support; peer review management; business model development; contract/license preparation; author copyright advisory; other author advisory; digitization; hosting of supplemental content; audio/video streaming

ADDITIONAL INFORMATION

Plans for expansion/future directions: In the future, UMass Amherst Libraries plans to collaborate with the University of Massachusetts Press to provide complete solutions for published scholarly work in both print and electronic formats. Topics to address include provision of joint editorial and production services. Content includes materials from the Open Education Initiative (OEI), which has saved students over $1 million in textbook costs and has resulted in innovative learning materials. A focus area for the upcoming year is outreach and expansion of services to the research centers and institutions on campus, so as to better serve and represent the strengths of UMass Amherst. Longer term goals include capturing undergraduate research, particularly for the Honors College and outstanding departmental projects.

UNIVERSITY OF MASSACHUSETTS MEDICAL SCHOOL
Lamar Soutter Library

Primary Unit: Research & Scholarly Communication Services

Primary Contact: Rebecca Reznik-Zellen
Head of Research & Scholarly Communication Services
508-856-6810
rebecca.reznik-zellen@umassmed.edu

Website: escholarship.umassmed.edu

PROGRAM OVERVIEW

Mission statement: eScholarship@UMMS is a freely available digital archive and publishing system offering worldwide access to the research and scholarly work of the University of Massachusetts Medical School community. The goal is to bring together the University's scholarly output in order to enhance its visibility and accessibility, and to serve as a portfolio for institutional successes. We help individual researchers and departments organize and disseminate their research beyond the walls of the Medical School by archiving publications, posters, presentations, and other materials they produce in their scholarly pursuits. Our publishing services—including open access, peer-reviewed electronic journals, student dissertations and theses, and conference proceedings—highlight the works of University of Massachusetts Medical School authors and others.

Year publishing activities began: 2007

Organization: services are distributed across library units/departments

Total FTE in support of publishing activities: professional staff (1); paraprofessional staff (.5)

Funding sources (%): library operating budget (80); grants (20)

PUBLISHING ACTIVITIES

Library publications in 2015: campus-based faculty-driven journals (3); textbooks (1); faculty conference papers and proceedings (228); student conference papers and proceedings (35); newsletters (1); ETDs (66)

Media formats: text; images; audio; video; data

Disciplinary specialties: library science; psychiatry/mental health research; neurology; clinical and translational science; life sciences

Top publications: *Journal of eScience Librarianship* (journal); ETDs; *Psychiatry Information in Brief* (journal); *Neurological Bulletin* (journal); *A History of the University of Massachusetts Medical School* (monograph)

Percentage of journals that are peer reviewed: 100

Internal partners: campus departments or programs; individual faculty; graduate students

Publishing platform(s): bepress (Digital Commons)

Digital preservation strategy: in-house; digital preservation services under discussion

Additional services: copyediting; marketing; outreach; training; metadata; notification of A&I sources; ISSN registry; DOI assignment/allocation of identifiers; open URL support; dataset management; peer review management; author copyright advisory; other author advisory; digitization; hosting of supplemental content; audio/video streaming; other

ADDITIONAL INFORMATION
Plans for expansion/future directions: Collaborating with additional departments within the medical school; incorporating more multimedia; continuing to develop and implement services to accommodate research datasets.

HIGHLIGHTED PUBLICATION

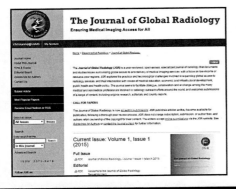

The *Journal of Global Radiology* (*JGR*) is a peer-reviewed, open-access, specialized journal of radiology that documents and studies issues surrounding global access to and delivery of medical imaging services, with a focus on low-income or resource-poor regions.

escholarship.umassmed.edu/jgr

UNIVERSITY OF MIAMI
University of Miami Libraries

Primary Unit: Digital Strategies

Primary Contact: Jason Cohen
Repository and Collection Assessment Coordinator
305-284-9169
j.cohen4@miami.edu

PROGRAM OVERVIEW
Mission statement: The University of Miami Libraries provides infrastructure and support for publishing and disseminating research and scholarship from our faculty and students.

Year publishing activities began: 2009

Organization: centralized library publishing unit/department

Total FTE in support of publishing activities: professional staff (1.5)

Funding sources (%): library materials budget (50); library operating budget (50)

PUBLISHING ACTIVITIES
Library publications in 2015: campus-based faculty-driven journals (1); ETDs (300)

Media formats: text; images; audio; video; data

Disciplinary specialties: Caribbean studies; music

Top publications: *Anthurium: A Caribbean Studies Journal* (journal); ETDs

Percentage of journals that are peer reviewed: 100

Internal partners: campus departments or programs; individual faculty

Publishing platform(s): bepress (Digital Commons)

Digital preservation strategy: AP Trust; DPN; in-house; digital preservation services under discussion

Additional services: training; DOI assignment/allocation of identifiers; author copyright advisory; other author advisory; digitization; hosting of supplemental content

ADDITIONAL INFORMATION

Plans for expansion/future directions: We hope to add more journals and provide greater support for monographs.

UNIVERSITY OF MICHIGAN
University Library

Library
Publishing
Coalition

FOUNDER

Primary Unit: Michigan Publishing
mpublishing@umich.edu

Primary Contact: Charles Watkinson
Associate University Librarian for Publishing
734-936-0452
watkinc@umich.edu

Website: www.publishing.umich.edu

Social media: @M_Publishing

PROGRAM OVERVIEW
Mission statement: Michigan Publishing is the hub of scholarly publishing at the University of Michigan, and is a part of its dynamic and innovative University Library. We publish scholarly and educational materials in a range of formats for wide dissemination and permanent preservation. We also provide publishing services to the University of Michigan community and beyond, and advocate for the broadest possible access to scholarship everywhere.

Year publishing activities began: 2001

Organization: centralized library publishing unit/department

Total FTE in support of publishing activities: professional staff (12)

Funding sources (%): library operating budget (70); sales revenue (30)

PUBLISHING ACTIVITIES
Library publications in 2015: campus-based faculty-driven journals (10); campus-based student-driven journals (1); journals produced under contract/ MOU for external groups (18); monographs (6); conference proceedings (7); textbooks (1); technical/research reports (50); ETDs (200); undergraduate capstones/honors theses (80); digital projects

Library-administered university press publications in 2015: 90 books

Media formats: text; images; audio; video; data

Disciplinary specialties: philosophy; Asian studies; information studies; medicine

Top publications: *Philosophers' Imprint* (journal); *Journal of Electronic Publishing* (journal); *Trans-Asia Photography Review* (journal); *Michigan Journal of Community Service Learning* (journal)

Percentage of journals that are peer reviewed: 79

Internal partners: campus departments or programs; individual faculty; graduate students; undergraduate students

External partners: Lever Press; American Council of Learned Societies

University press partners: University of Michigan Press

Publishing platform(s): DSpace; Hydra/Fedora; WordPress; locally developed software; DLXS; Drupal

Digital preservation strategy: HathiTrust; in-house

Additional services: graphic design (print or web); print-on-demand; typesetting; copy-editing; marketing; outreach; training; analytics; cataloging; metadata ISSN registry; ISBN registry; DOI assignment/allocation of identifiers; contract/license preparation; author copyright advisory; other author advisory

ADDITIONAL INFORMATION

Plans for expansion/future directions: In the coming years, we will execute further integration of our library and university press operations, and expand our publishing services program target to meet the needs of our campus community.

UNIVERSITY OF MINNESOTA
University of Minnesota Libraries

Primary Unit: Open Scholarship & Publishing Services
libpubs@umn.edu

Primary Contact: Kate McCready
Director of Content Services
612-626-4357
mccre008@umn.edu

Website: www.lib.umn.edu/publishing

PROGRAM OVERVIEW

Mission statement: The Open Scholarship & Publishing Services unit is located within the new and growing Content Services Department. Content Services is comprised of two units: Interlibrary Loan, which provides support for and information about resource sharing; and Open Scholarship and Publishing Services, which integrates Copyright Information Services, Copyright Permissions Services, and Publishing Services. Publishing Services provides support for the creation, production, and dissemination of the University's faculty- and instructor-produced digital scholarship. The Copyright Information Services provides education and consultation services on copyright, licensing, and other intellectual property issues for the campus community. Copyright Permissions Services handles the rights management work for content reuse by our faculty, staff, and students. The major objectives for the department are to conceptualize, implement, and promote sustainable services for content creation and publishing for scholarly and creative works for the campus community; integrate and anchor copyright services within the new department by maintaining and expanding current education, outreach, and consultation services; and, finally, anchoring and operationalizing scholarly communications activities within the department.

Year publishing activities began: 2006; 2014

Organization: centralized library publishing unit/department

Total FTE in support of publishing activities: professional staff (2); paraprofessional staff (1)

Funding sources (%): library operating budget (50); endowment income (25); library materials budget (25)

PUBLISHING ACTIVITIES

Library publications in 2015: campus based faculty-driven journals (7); textbooks (2); faculty conference papers and proceedings (2,520); ETDs (4,691)

Media formats: text; images; audio; video; data; concept maps, modeling, maps, or other visualizations

Percentage of journals that are peer reviewed: 50

Internal partners: campus departments or programs; individual faculty

Publishing platform(s): bepress (Digital Commons); CONTENTdm; DSpace; WordPress

Digital preservation strategy: CLOCKSS; DuraCloud; HathiTrust; Portico; digital preservation services under discussion

Additional services: outreach; training; notification of A&I sources; dataset management; author copyright advisory; digitization; hosting of supplemental content

ADDITIONAL INFORMATION

Plans for expansion/future directions: Although many publishing services have existed before, the establishment of the new department coalesced many existing services into a single unit while expanding other operations, most notably publishing services. In the future, the department will grow to incorporate an existing university permissions center and to more fully anchor open scholarship solutions.

HIGHLIGHTED PUBLICATION

The Interdisciplinary Journal of Partnership Studies (IJPS) shares scholarship and creates connections for cultural transformation to build a world in which all relationships, institutions, policies and organizations are based on principles of partnership.

pubs.lib.umn.edu/ijps/vol1/iss1

UNIVERSITY OF NEBRASKA-LINCOLN
University of Nebraska-Lincoln Libraries

Primary Unit: Office of Scholarly Communications
proyster@unl.edu

Primary Contact: Paul Royster
Coordinator of Scholarly Communications
402-472-3628
proyster@unl.edu

Website: digitalcommons.unl.edu

PROGRAM OVERVIEW
Mission statement: Zea Books is the digital and on-demand publishing operation of the University of Nebraska-Lincoln Libraries. Its mission is to publish academic works (books, journals, multimedia) by scholars who are either affiliated with the University of Nebraska-Lincoln or are working in research areas of significant interest at UNL. Zea Books provides an innovative way for faculty to promote and disseminate their scholarly research. The imprint also helps foster the University of Nebraska-Lincoln's commitment to the future of scholarly communications.

Year publishing activities began: 2005

Organization: centralized library publishing unit/department

Total FTE in support of publishing activities: professional staff (0.4); undergraduates (0.1)

Funding sources (%): library operating budget (98); sales revenue (2)

PUBLISHING ACTIVITIES
Library publications in 2015: campus-based faculty-driven journals (6); campus-based student-driven journals (3); journals produced under contract/MOU for external groups (3); monographs (8); technical/research reports (25); faculty conference papers and proceedings (1); student conference papers and proceedings (2); newsletters (6); ETDs (400); undergraduate capstones/honors theses (40)

Media formats: text; images; audio; video; data; concept maps, modeling, maps, or other visualizations

Disciplinary specialties: ornithology; parasitology; Holocaust studies; entomology; horticulture

Top publications: *Loris Malaguzzi and the Teachers: Dialogues on Collaboration and Conflict among Children, Reggio Emilia 1990* (monograph); *At Home and at Large in the Great Plains: Essays and Memories; Historical Common Names of Great Plains Plants* (2 vols.) (monograph); *Syntagma Musicum II: De Organographia, Parts III–V with Index* (monograph); "Sinners in the Hands of an Angry God" (sermon)

Percentage of journals that are peer reviewed: 100

Internal partners: campus departments or programs; individual faculty; graduate students; undergraduate students

External partners: Nebraska Academy of Sciences; Center for Systemic Entomology; National Collegiate Honors Council; Nebraska Ornithologists Union

Publishing platform(s): bepress (Digital Commons)

Additional services: graphic design (print or web); print-on-demand; typesetting; copy-editing; outreach; training; analytics; cataloging; metadata; compiling indexes and/or TOCs; ISSN registry; ISBN registry; peer review management; author copyright advisory; other author advisory; digitization; image services; data visualization; hosting of supplemental content

ADDITIONAL INFORMATION

Additional information: Enquiries welcome in all fields, from all sources. Easy terms, short turnarounds. Spanish and French text or translations accommodated. We do not require Budapest-style open access; authors may apply CC licenses if they wish. Our publications are free public access but copyright remains with author.

Plans for expansion/future directions: Hope to expand staff and titles by 25 to 50 percent in next 1–2 years.

UNIVERSITY OF NEW ORLEANS
Earl K. Long Library

Primary Unit: Scholarly Communication
scholarworks@uno.edu

Primary Contact: Jeanne Pavy
Scholarly Communication Librarian
504-280-6547
jpavy@uno.edu

Website: scholarworks.uno.edu

PROGRAM OVERVIEW
Mission statement: The UNO Library offers ScholarWorks@UNO as a publishing platform for faculty and student scholarship. Our goal is to provide the tools and support for the broadest possible dissemination of campus research and creative work, thereby fulfilling a key element of the University mission: the promotion of research excellence. In so doing, we provide opportunities for students to engage with scholarly communications issues and take their first steps as scholars in their respective disciplines. Our broad range of publications, which currently include a student-edited, peer-reviewed literary journal, conference proceedings, working papers, technical reports, and student theses and dissertations, engage both our local community and the worldwide audience of readers and scholars. In the future we hope to host even more kinds of scholarly and creative work, including datasets and multimedia content. By combining a dynamic publishing platform with expert support, we can contribute to a more open and innovative scholarly communication system that facilitates discovery, collaboration, and the advancement of knowledge.

Year publishing activities began: 2000

Organization: centralized library publishing unit/department

Total FTE in support of publishing activities: professional staff (1)

Funding sources (%): library operating budget (35); non-library campus budget (15); charitable contributions/Friends of the Library organizations (50)

PUBLISHING ACTIVITIES
Library publications in 2015: campus-based student-driven journals (1); technical/research reports (15); faculty conference papers and proceedings (1); student conference papers and proceedings (1); newsletters (1); ETDs (179); undergraduate capstones/honors theses (13)

Media formats: text; images; video

Disciplinary specialties: creative writing; marine engineering; urban studies; hazards assessment and response

Top publications: University of New Orleans Theses & Dissertations; University of New Orleans Senior Honors Theses; *Ellipsis: A Journal of Art, Ideas, and Literature* (journal); Center for Hazards Assessment, Response, and Technology Publications; Planning and Urban Studies Reports & Presentations

Percentage of journals that are peer reviewed: 100

Internal partners: campus departments or programs; individual faculty; graduate students; undergraduate students

External partners: Southern Universities Research Association (SURA)

Publishing platform(s): bepress (Digital Commons)

Digital preservation strategy: in-house

Additional services: outreach; training; metadata; ISSN registry; peer review management; author copyright advisory; hosting of supplemental content

ADDITIONAL INFORMATION
Plans for expansion/future directions: We hope to increase the number of journals and conferences published and also to begin publishing datasets.

UNIVERSITY OF NORTH CAROLINA AT CHAPEL HILL
University Library

Primary Unit: Library & Information Technology

Primary Contact: Will Owen
Associate University Librarian for Technical Services and Systems
919-962-8026
owen@email.unc.edu

PROGRAM OVERVIEW
Mission statement: The Library has historically published, in print, specialized monographs on topics related to the University or Library. We publish ETDs electronically, and provide digital editions and original scholarly interpretations, in support of research and instruction, with a special emphasis on the American South.

Year publishing activities began: 1995

Organization: services are primarily concentrated in the Library, distributed across departments/units

Total FTE in support of publishing activities: professional staff (1); paraprofessional staff (1); graduate students (0.5)

Funding sources (%): library operating budget (100)

PUBLISHING ACTIVITIES
Library publications in 2015: ETDs (1379); undergraduate capstones/honors theses (479); digital humanities research projects

Media formats: text; images; audio; video; data; concept maps, modeling, maps, or other visualizations; visualizations

Disciplinary specialties: American South; Latin American studies (forthcoming)

Internal partners: campus departments or programs; individual faculty

Publishing platform(s): CONTENTdm; Fedora; WordPress; locally developed software

Digital preservation strategy: Archive-It; HathiTrust; in-house; The Carolina Digital Repository and Curator's Workbench are locally developed software built on Fedora and iRODS

Additional services: print-on-demand; training; cataloging; metadata; author copyright advisory; digitization; hosting of supplemental content

ADDITIONAL INFORMATION

Plans for expansion/future directions: New this year, we are undertaking a project with the UNC Press and the Institute for the Study of the American South to jointly produce a new series of short monographs in the range of 20,000–40,000 words to be published electronically. Estimated output is initially one or two titles a year, with first titles appearing in 2015. Collaborating with researchers on archiving, preserving, and publishing research data; collaborating with UNC Press for print-on-demand publications.

UNIVERSITY OF NORTH CAROLINA AT CHARLOTTE

J. Murrey Atkins Library

Primary Unit: Digital Initiatives
atkins-dsl@uncc.edu

Primary Contact: Somaly Kim Wu
Digital Scholarship Librarian
704-687-1112
skimwu@uncc.edu

Website: dsl.uncc.edu

PROGRAM OVERVIEW

Mission statement: We support the publication of scholarly journals online, and assist journal editors with the management, editorial work, and production of their scholarly journals. The DSL offers journal hosting support services to UNC Charlotte faculty. Our services are built on the Open Journal System (OJS) journal management software that facilitates the publication of online peer-reviewed journals. DSL services include platform software hosting, updates, and copyright consulting.

Year publishing activities began: 2012

Organization: centralized library publishing unit/department

Total FTE in support of publishing activities: professional staff (1)

Funding sources (%): library operating budget (100)

PUBLISHING ACTIVITIES

Library publications in 2015: monographs (1)

Media formats: text

Disciplinary specialties: education; psychology; urban education; applied educational and policy research

Top publications: *NHSA Dialog* (journal); *Urban Education Research and Policy Annuals* (journal); *Undergraduate Journal of Psychology* (journal); *Journal of Applied Educational and Policy Research* (journal)

Percentage of journals that are peer reviewed: 100

Internal partners: individual faculty

Publishing platform(s): OJS

Digital preservation strategy: digital preservation services under discussion

Additional services: graphic design (print or web); ISSN registry dataset management; author copyright advisory

ADDITIONAL INFORMATION
Plans for expansion/future directions: Building an institutional repository on the Islandora platform; expansion of services to include support for conference paper and proceedings (OCS) and e-textbooks (OMP) under discussion.

UNIVERSITY OF NORTH CAROLINA AT GREENSBORO

University Libraries

Primary Unit: Collections and Scholarly Communications

Primary Contact: Beth Bernhardt
Assistant Dean for Collections and Scholarly Communications
336-256-1210
brbernha@uncg.edu

PROGRAM OVERVIEW
Mission statement: still in development

Year publishing activities began: 2004

Organization: services are distributed across library units/departments

Total FTE in support of publishing activities: library staff (0.5)

Funding sources (%): other (100)

PUBLISHING ACTIVITIES
Library publications in 2015: campus-based faculty-driven journals (7); journals produced under contract/MOU for external groups (1); technical/research reports (23); faculty conference papers and proceedings (32); databases (4); ETDs (2,083)

Media formats: text; images; audio; video; data; concept maps, modeling, maps, or other visualizations; multimedia/interactive content

Disciplinary specialties: public health; education; nursing; sociology

Top publications: *The International Journal of Critical Pedagogy* (journal); *Journal of Backcountry Studies* (journal); *Journal of Learning Spaces* (journal); *Partnerships: A Journal of Service-Learning and Civic Engagement* (journal); *Archival Practice* (journal)

Percentage of journals that are peer reviewed: 85

Internal partners: campus departments or programs; individual faculty; graduate students; undergraduate students

Publishing platform(s): CONTENTdm; OJS/OCS/OMP; locally developed software

Digital preservation strategy: HathiTrust; in-house; digital preservation services under discussion

Additional services: training; analytics; cataloging; metadata; author copyright advisory; other author advisory; digitization; hosting of supplemental content

ADDITIONAL INFORMATION

Plans for expansion/future directions: Hosting OJS for other regional libraries; supporting faculty in new scholarly media, such as database and UI design, web pages, and usability.

HIGHLIGHTED PUBLICATION

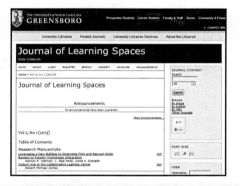

A peer-reviewed, open-access journal published biannually, *The Journal of Learning Spaces* provides a scholarly, multidisciplinary forum for research articles, case studies, book reviews, and position pieces related to all aspects of learning space design, operation, pedagogy, and assessment in higher education.

partnershipsjournal.org/index.php/jls

UNIVERSITY OF NORTH TEXAS
Libraries

Primary Unit: Scholarly Publishing Services

Primary Contact: Kevin S. Hawkins
Director for Academic Publishing Transformation
940-565-2015
Kevin.Hawkins@unt.edu

Website: www.library.unt.edu/scholarly-publishing

PROGRAM OVERVIEW
Year publishing activities began: 2009

Organization: services are distributed across library units/departments

Total FTE in support of publishing activities: professional staff (1.98); paraprofessional staff (0.06); undergraduates (1.50)

Funding sources (%): library operating budget (61%); charge backs (39%)

PUBLISHING ACTIVITIES
Library publications in 2015: campus-based student-driven journals (1); monographs (1); ETDs (4,500)

Library-administered university press publications in 2015: monographs (25)

Media formats: images; audio; video; data; multimedia/interactive content

Top publications: *Economics: From the Dismal Science to the Moral Science: The Moral Economics of Kendall P. Cochran* (monograph); *The Eagle Feather* (journal)

Percentage of journals that are peer reviewed: 100

Internal partners: campus departments or programs; individual faculty; graduate students; undergraduate students

University press partners: University of North Texas Press

Publishing platform(s): Drupal; OJS; WordPress; locally developed software

Digital preservation strategy: LOCKSS; MetaArchive; in-house

Additional services: graphic design (print or web); print-on-demand; typesetting; copy-editing; analytics; cataloging; metadata; compiling indexes and/or TOCs; ISSN registry; ISBN registry; DOI assignment/allocation of identifiers; peer review management; contract/license preparation; author copyright advisory; other author advisory; digitization; hosting of supplemental content; audio/video streaming

ADDITIONAL INFORMATION

Plans for expansion/future directions: We hope to make select titles from the Portal to Texas History available for sale using print-on-demand technology. We also hope to partner with our campus's learning-technology support unit on an initiative to support textbook alternatives.

HIGHLIGHTED PUBLICATION

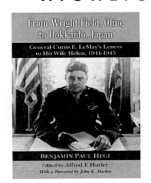

LeMay's activities in World War II are well-documented, but his personal history is less thoroughly recorded. Throughout the war he wrote hundreds of letters to his wife, Helen, and daughter, Jane. They are published for the first time in this volume, weaved together with meticulously researched narrative essays and supplemented with extensive footnotes.

www.library.unt.edu/eagle-editions/lemay-001-4

171

UNIVERSITY OF OKLAHOMA
University of Oklahoma Libraries

Primary Unit: Repository Services

Primary Contact: David Corbly
Director, Repository Services
405-325-6878
dcorbly@ou.edu

PROGRAM OVERVIEW
Mission statement: The University of Oklahoma Libraries supports platforms for open access journal and book publishing. We seek publishing partners who: wish to publish open access journals; wish to publish open access books in the history of science; utilize an internationally/nationally recognized editorial board; have the resources and staff to publish in a timely manner on a regular schedule; seek to publish original scholarly content; are selective in accepting quality content for publication via a rigorous peer-review process.

Year publishing activities began: 2013

Organization: services are distributed across library units/departments

Total FTE in support of publishing activities: professional staff (1)

Funding sources (%): library materials budget (100)

PUBLISHING ACTIVITIES
Library publications in 2015: campus-based faculty-driven journals (1); ETDs (215)

Library-administered university press publications in 2015: campus-based faculty-driven journals (1)

Media formats: text

Disciplinary specialties: children's and young adult literature; American politics; higher education athletics

Top publications: *American Review of Politics* (journal); *Study and Scrutiny: Research on Young Adult Literature* (journal)

Percentage of journals that are peer reviewed: 100

Internal partners: campus departments or programs

Publishing platform(s): DSpace; Islandora; OJS

Digital preservation strategy: Amazon Glacier; Amazon S3; Archive-It; in-house

Additional services: graphic design (print or web); marketing; outreach; training; analytics; cataloging; metadata; notification of A&I sources; ISSN registry; DOI assignment/allocation of identifiers; open URL support; dataset management; author copyright advisory; digitization

UNIVERSITY OF OREGON
University of Oregon Libraries

Primary Unit: Digital Scholarship Center
dsc@uoregon.edu

Primary Contact: John Russell
Scholarly Communications Librarian
541-346-2689
johnruss@uoregon.edu

Website: library.uoregon.edu/digitalscholarship

PROGRAM OVERVIEW
Mission statement: The Digital Scholarship Center (DSC) collaborates with faculty and students to transform research and scholarly communication using new media and digital technologies. Based on a foundation of access, sharing, and preservation, the DSC provides digital asset management, digital preservation, training, consultations, and tools for digital scholarship.

Year publishing activities began: 2003

Organization: centralized library publishing unit/department

Total FTE in support of publishing activities: professional staff (0.5); paraprofessional staff (0.75); undergraduate students (0.2)

Funding sources (%): library operating budget (100)

PUBLISHING ACTIVITIES
Library publications in 2015: campus-based faculty-driven journals (4); campus-based student-driven journals (1); ETDs (325); undergraduate capstones/honors theses (94)

Media formats: text; images; audio; video; data; concept maps, modeling, maps, or other visualizations; multimedia/interactive content

Disciplinary specialties: humanities; gender studies; archaeology

Percentage of journals that are peer reviewed: 100

Internal partners: campus departments or programs; individual faculty; graduate students; undergraduate students

External partners: Fembot Collective

Publishing platform(s): CONTENTdm; DSpace; OJS; WordPress

Digital preservation strategy: in-house

Additional services: outreach; training; cataloging; metadata; ISSN registry; ISBN registry; DOI assignment/allocation of identifiers; author copyright advisory; hosting of supplemental content; audio/video streaming

UNIVERSITY OF PITTSBURGH
University Library System

Primary Unit: Office of Scholarly Communication and Publishing
oscp@mail.pitt.edu

Primary Contact: Timothy S. Deliyannides
Director, Office of Scholarly Communication and Publishing
412-648-3254
tsd@pitt.edu

Website: www.library.pitt.edu/e-journals

Social media: @OSCP_Pitt

PROGRAM OVERVIEW

Mission statement: The University Library System, University of Pittsburgh offers a full range of publishing services for a variety of content types, specializing in scholarly journals and subject-based open access repositories. Because we are committed to helping research communities share knowledge and ideas through open and responsible collaboration, we subsidize the costs of electronic publishing and provide incentives to promote open access to scholarly research. We strive to promote scholarly publishing at a very low cost; allow easy collaboration among authors, editors, and reviewers regardless of location; and enhance the visibility, discoverability, and navigation of our publications. We actively develop and employ innovative and sustainable technologies to accelerate knowledge production, measure the impact of our research publications, and demonstrate return on investment. We are seeking partners around the world who share our commitment to open access to scholarly research information. Our skilled staff will help you turn your ideas into reality to produce an online academic journal of the highest quality at very low cost. To learn more, visit www.library.pitt.edu/e-journals.

Year publishing activities began: 1999

Organization: centralized library publishing unit/department

Total FTE in support of publishing activities: professional staff (4); paraprofessional staff (0.5); graduate students (0.5); undergraduate students (0.5)

Funding sources (%): library operating budget (75); charge backs (25)

PUBLISHING ACTIVITIES

Library publications in 2015: campus-based faculty-driven journals (11); campus-based student-driven journals (9); journals produced under contract/ MOU for external groups (17); monographs (7); technical/research reports (2,530); faculty conference papers and proceedings (250); ETDs (640); undergraduate capstones/honors theses (109); government documents (10,199); unpublished manuscripts (381)

Media formats: text; images; audio; video; data; concept maps, modeling, maps, or other visualizations; multimedia/interactive content

Disciplinary specialties: Latin American studies; European studies; history and philosophy of science; law; health sciences

Top publications: *Revista Iberoamericana* (journal); *University of Pittsburgh Law Review* (journal); *Archive of European Integration* (document repository); *PhilSci-Archive* (preprint repository); *International Journal of Telerehabilitation* (journal)

Percentage of journals that are peer reviewed: 100

Internal partners: campus departments or programs; individual faculty; graduate students; undergraduate students

External partners: American Forensic Association; American Hungarian Educators Association; American Sociological Association: Political Economy of the World-System Section; Association for Anthropology and Gerontology; Brunel University; European Union Studies Association; Fonds Ricoeur; Grupo Biblios; Institute for Linguistic Evidence; Institute for Quantitative Social Science, Harvard University; Institute of Integrative Omics and Applied Biotechnology; Institute of Public Health, Bangalore, India; Instituto Internacional de Literatura Iberoamericana; International Network of the Development of Library and Information Science; Kadir Has University; Konsorsium Perguruan Tinggi Indonesia–Pittsburgh (KPTIP); LAPS/ENSP Oswaldo Cruz Foundation LAPS; Motivational Interviewing Network of Trainers (MINT); Nazarbayev University, Astana, Kazakhstan; Pennsylvania Library Association, College and Research Division; Société Américaine de Philosophie de Langue Française; Society for Ricoeur Studies; TALE: The Association for Linguistic Evidence; University of Chapeco, Department of Anthropology; University of Kingston Centre for Modern European Philosophy

University press partners: University of Pittsburgh Press

Publishing platform(s): EPrints; Fedora; Islandora; OJS; OMP; WordPress; locally developed software

Digital preservation strategy: discoverygarden; HathiTrust; LOCKSS Alliance; PKP Private LOCKSS Network; in-house

Additional services: graphic design (print or web); print-on-demand; typesetting; marketing; outreach; training; analytics; cataloging; metadata; compiling indexes and/or TOCs; notification of A&I sources; ISSN registry; ISBN registry; applying for Cataloging-in-Publication Data; DOI assignment/allocation of identifiers; dataset management; business model development; contract/license preparation; author copyright advisory; other author advisory; digitization hosting of supplemental content; audio/video streaming; article level metrics (traditional and altmetrics)

ADDITIONAL INFORMATION
Plans for expansion/future directions: Through our development partnership with Plum Analytics, we offer traditional and alternative metrics at the article level through PlumX for all our journals and repositories.

HIGHLIGHTED PUBLICATION

Central Asian Journal of Global Health

The Central Asian Journal of Global Health is aimed at researchers in the fields of public health and medicine focusing on Central Asian countries, a geographic region that is often not sufficiently highlighted by existing journals.

cajgh.pitt.edu

UNIVERSITY OF PUGET SOUND
Collins Memorial Library

Primary Unit: Digital Collections
soundideas@pugetsound.edu

Primary Contact: Benjamin Tucker
Librarian
253-879-3667
btucker@pugetsound.edu

Website: soundideas.pugetsound.edu

PROGRAM OVERVIEW
Mission statement: Sound Ideas represents the scholarship and creative works of the faculty, staff, and students of the University of Puget Sound. Sound Ideas, organized and made accessible by Collins Memorial Library, demonstrates our institutional commitment to helping enrich the global academic community through sharing and collaboration.

Organization: centralized library publishing unit/department

Total FTE in support of publishing activities: professional staff (0.1); undergraduate students (0.25)

Funding sources (%): library operating budget (100)

PUBLISHING ACTIVITIES
Library publications in 2015: campus-based student-driven journals (1); faculty conference papers and proceedings (1); student conference papers and proceedings (2); ETDs (1); undergraduate capstones/honors theses (7)

Media formats: text; images; video

Disciplinary specialties: neuroscience

Top publications: School of Occupational Therapy theses (theses); *Puget Sound Trail* (newspaper); *Sound Neuroscience: An Undergraduate Neuroscience Journal* (journal); Economics theses (theses)

Percentage of journals that are peer reviewed: 0

Internal partners: campus departments or programs; individual faculty

Publishing platform(s): bepress (Digital Commons)

Digital preservation strategy: digital preservation services under discussion

Additional services: outreach; metadata; author copyright advisory; audio/video streaming

ADDITIONAL INFORMATION

Plans for expansion/future directions: Continued growth of thesis and undergraduate capstone collections; development of original journals.

UNIVERSITY OF RICHMOND
Boatwright Memorial Library

Primary Unit: Scholarly Communications
lmcculle@richmond.edu

Primary Contact: Lucretia McCulley
Head, Scholarly Communications
804-289-8670
lmcculle@richmond.edu

Website: scholarship.richmond.edu

PROGRAM OVERVIEW
Mission statement: Through the university's institutional repository, UR Scholarship, we seek to publish and archive faculty and student research, conference and symposium material, and art exhibition catalogs. We publish and archive undergraduate honors theses and master's program theses. We are also in the process of hosting three journals related to the University of Richmond.

Year publishing activities began: 2013

Organization: services are distributed across library units/departments

Total FTE in support of publishing activities: professional staff (1); paraprofessional staff (2)

Funding sources (%): library operating budget (100)

PUBLISHING ACTIVITIES
Library publications in 2015: campus-based student-driven journals (1); journals produced under contract/MOU for external groups (2)

Media formats: text; images; audio; video

Disciplinary specialties: leadership studies; business; arts and sciences; professional and continuing studies

Top publications: master's theses (theses); honors theses (theses); Robins Case Network (case studies repository); faculty publications

Percentage of journals that are peer reviewed: 30

Internal partners: campus departments or programs; individual faculty; undergraduate students

Publishing platform(s): bepress (Digital Commons)

Digital preservation strategy: digital preservation services under discussion

Additional services: marketing; outreach; training; metadata ISSN registry; author copyright advisory

ADDITIONAL INFORMATION
Plans for expansion/future directions: We will continue to seek collaborations with faculty, staff and students on campus to publish journals or other research materials related to the University of Richmond.

UNIVERSITY OF SAN DIEGO
Copley Library

Primary Unit: Special Collections and Archives

Primary Contact: Kelly Riddle
Digital Initiatives Librarian
649-260-6850
kriddle@sandiego.edu

PROGRAM OVERVIEW
Mission statement: Copley Library at the University of San Diego is dedicated to providing publishing services that disseminate work created at the university so that it is readily discoverable, openly accessible, preserved, and sustainable. The library's publishing program serves to advance scholarly conversations and foster intellectual collaboration both locally and globally.

Year publishing activities began: 2013

Organization: centralized library publishing unit/department

Total FTE in support of publishing activities: professional staff (1); paraprofessional staff (0.5); undergraduate students (0.5)

Funding sources (%): library operating budget (100)

PUBLISHING ACTIVITIES
Media formats: text; images; audio; video; data; concept maps, modeling, maps, or other visualizations

Internal partners: campus departments or programs; individual faculty; graduate students; undergraduate students

Publishing platform(s): bepress (Digital Commons)

Digital preservation strategy: digital preservation services under discussion

Additional services: training; cataloging; metadata; author copyright advisory; digitization

UNIVERSITY OF SOUTH FLORIDA
USF Library

Primary Unit: Academic Resources
scholarcommons@usf.edu

Primary Contact: Jason Boczar
Digital Scholarship and Publishing Librarian
813-974-5505
jboczar@usf.edu

Website: scholarcommons.usf.edu

Social media: facebook.com/pages/USF-Scholar-Commons/260978313955466;
@scholarcommons

PROGRAM OVERVIEW

Mission statement: The USF Tampa Library strives to develop and encourage research collaboration and initiatives throughout all areas of campus. Members of the USF community are encouraged to deposit their research with Scholar Commons. We commit to assisting faculty, staff, and students in all stages of the deposit process, to managing their work to optimize access/readership, and to ensure long-term preservation. Long-term preservation and increasing accessibility will increase citation rates and highlight the research accomplishments of this campus. Scholar Commons will have a direct impact on the University's four strategic goals: student success, research innovation, sound financial management, and creating new partnerships.

Year publishing activities began: 2007

Organization: centralized library publishing unit/department

Total FTE in support of publishing activities: professional staff (1.5); paraprofessional staff (2); undergraduates (0.5)

Funding sources (%): library materials budget (40); library operating budget (60)

PUBLISHING ACTIVITIES

Library publications in 2015: campus-based faculty-driven journals (1); faculty conference papers and proceedings (26); newsletters (1); ETDs (213)

Media formats: text; images; audio; video; data; concept maps, modeling, maps, or other visualizations; multimedia/interactive content

184

Disciplinary specialties: geology and karst; literature; environmental sustainability; Holocaust and genocide; math/quantitative literature

Top publications: *Social Science Research: Principles, Methods, and Practices* (textbook); *Journal of Strategic Security* (journal); *International Journal of Speleology* (journal); *Numeracy: Advancing Education in Quantitative Literacy* (journal); ETDs

Percentage of journals that are peer reviewed: 80

Internal partners: campus departments or programs; individual faculty

External partners: Florida Holocaust Museum, National Cave and Karst Research Institute (NCKRI); Aphra Behn Society; Union Internationale de Spéléologie; Center for Conflict Management (CCM) of the National University of Rwanda (NUR); HenleyPutnam University; National Numeracy Network (NNN); IAVCEI Commission on Statistics in Volcanology (COSIV); Babeş-Bolyai University; National Center for Suburban Studies at Hofstra University; International Association of Genocide Scholars (IAGS)

Publishing platform(s): bepress (Digital Commons)

Digital preservation strategy: LOCKSS; Portico; in-house; bepress Digital Commons Private LOCKSS Network

Additional services: graphic design (print or web); typesetting; training; analytics; cataloging; metadata; compiling indexes and/or TOCs; notification of A&I sources; ISSN registry; ISBN registry; DOI assignment/allocation of identifiers; open URL support; dataset management; peer review managementcontract/license preparation; author copyright advisory; hosting of supplemental content

ADDITIONAL INFORMATION
Plans for expansion/future directions: Ingesting the USF FAIR CV Bank and expanding data content areas.

UNIVERSITY OF TENNESSEE
University of Tennessee Libraries

Primary Unit: Digital Production & Publishing/Newfound Press

Primary Contact: Holly Mercer
Associate Dean for Research & Scholarly Communication
865-974-6899
hollymercer@utk.edu

Website: www.newfoundpress.utk.edu; trace.tennessee.edu

Social media: @NewfoundPress

PROGRAM OVERVIEW

Mission statement: The University of Tennessee Libraries makes original, scholarly, and specialized works available worldwide. Newfound Press, the University Libraries digital imprint, advances the community of learning by experimenting with effective and open systems of scholarly communication. Drawing on the resources that the university has invested in digital library development, Newfound Press collaborates with authors and researchers to bring new forms of publication to an expanding scholarly universe. UT Libraries provides open access publishing services, copyright education, and services to help scholars meet new data management and sharing requirements. In addition, we create digital collections of regional and global importance to support research and teaching.

Year publishing activities began: 2005

Organization: centralized library publishing unit/department

Total FTE in support of publishing activities: professional staff (0.5); paraprofessional staff (1.6); graduate students (0.5)

Funding sources (%): library operating budget (99); sales revenue (1)

PUBLISHING ACTIVITIES

Library publications in 2015: campus-based faculty-driven journals (2); campus-based student-driven journals (5); journals produced under contract/MOU for external groups (2); monographs (3); ETDs (568); undergraduate capstones/honors theses (94)

Media formats: text; multimedia/interactive content

Disciplinary specialties: East Tennessee; Great Smoky Mountains; anthropology; sociology; law

Top publications: *Correspondence of James K. Polk, volume 12* (monograph); *From Cahokia to Larson to Moundville: Earth, World Renewal, and the Sacred in the Mississippian Social World of the Late Prehistoric Eastern Woodlands* (monograph); *The Fishes of Tennessee* (monograph); "The Impact of Colonialism on African Economic Development" (undergraduate thesis); "Recovery, Renewal, Reclaiming: Anthropological Research Toward Healing" (conference paper)

Percentage of journals that are peer reviewed: 64

Internal partners: campus departments or programs; individual faculty; graduate students; undergraduate students

External partners: Southern Anthropological Society; Music Theory Society of the Mid-Atlantic; Southeastern Fishes Council; National Council of Teachers of English

University press partners: University of Tennessee Press

Publishing platform(s): bepress (Digital Commons); locally developed software; Drupal

Digital preservation strategy: DuraCloud; MetaArchive; DPN

HIGHLIGHTED PUBLICATION

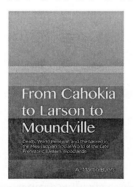

Noted archaeologist A. Martin Byers challenges assumptions about chiefdoms-dominance based hierarchical societies and offers a contrasting view by deconstructing the chiefdom model and offering instead an autonomous social world that focused on spiritual renewal and sacred rituals.

dx.doi.org/10.7290/V76Q1V59

Additional services: graphic design (print or web); typesetting; copy-editing; outreach; training; analytics; cataloging; metadata; notification of A&I sources; ISBN registry; applying for Cataloging-in-Publication Data; DOI assignment/ allocation of identifiers; peer review management; contract/license preparation; author copyright advisory; digitization; audio/video streaming

ADDITIONAL INFORMATION

Additional information: Newfound Press is not considering unsolicited manuscripts at this time.

Plans for expansion/future directions: We will focus on publishing manuscripts and other materials from the Libraries' special collections. We also are exploring how we can help certify the products of digital humanities research.

UNIVERSITY OF TEXAS AT ARLINGTON
University of Texas at Arlington Libraries

Primary Contact: Faedra Wills
Digital Project Librarian
817-272-1320
wills@uta.edu

PROGRAM OVERVIEW
Mission statement: To provide Open Access and increase the resonance of scholarship at the University of Texas at Arlington.

Year publishing activities began: 2007

Organization: services are distributed across library units/departments

Total FTE in support of publishing activities: professional staff (1); paraprofessional staff (1)

Funding sources (%): library operating budget (100)

PUBLISHING ACTIVITIES
Library publications in 2015: campus-based faculty-driven journals (1); campus-based student-driven journals (1); journals produced under contract/MOU for external groups (1); monographs (1); faculty conference papers and proceedings (1); newsletters (1); ETDs (400); image/metadata datasets (18069)

Media formats: text; images; audio; video; multimedia/interactive content

Percentage of journals that are peer reviewed: 100

Internal partners: campus departments or programs; individual faculty; graduate students

Publishing platform(s): DSpace; OJS; OCS; Omeka

Digital preservation strategy: in-house

Additional services: graphic design (print or web); outreach; training; analytics; cataloging; metadata; ISSN registry; ISBN registry; contract/license preparation; author copyright advisory; digitization; image services

ADDITIONAL INFORMATION

Plans for expansion/future directions: Saturation of scholarly communication education and support for faculty, graduate, and undergraduate students.

UNIVERSITY OF VIRGINIA
University of Virginia Library

Primary Unit: Content Stewardship

Primary Contact: Ellen Ramsey
Director, Scholarly Repository Services
434-243-7079
ecr2c@virginia.edu

PROGRAM OVERVIEW
Mission statement: The UVa institutional repository, Libra, makes publications available to the world and provides safe and secure storage for the scholarly output of the UVa community. Efforts are underway to expand Library publishing activities beyond the institutional repository model to include UVa-hosted journals and other scholarly outputs.

Year publishing activities began: 2010

Organization: centralized library publishing unit/department

Total FTE in support of publishing activities: professional staff (2); paraprofessional staff (1)

Funding sources (%): library operating budget (75); grants (25)

PUBLISHING ACTIVITIES
Library publications in 2015: monographs (4); technical/research reports (4); ETDs (485); undergraduate capstones/honors theses (2)

Media formats: text; images; audio; video; data

Internal partners: campus departments or programs; individual faculty; graduate students

University press partners: University of Virginia Press

Publishing platform(s): Hydra/Fedora; WordPress; locally developed software

Digital preservation strategy: AP Trust

Additional services: analytics; cataloging; metadata; dataset management; author copyright advisory; digitization; hosting of supplemental content

ADDITIONAL INFORMATION

Plans for expansion/future directions: Exploratory efforts are underway to expand Library publishing services to UVa-hosted journals and emerging modes of faculty scholarship.

UNIVERSITY OF WASHINGTON
University of Washington Libraries

Primary Unit: Digital Initiatives

Primary Contact: Ann Lally
Head, Digital Initiatives
206-685-1473
alally@uw.edu

Website: researchworks.lib.washington.edu

PROGRAM OVERVIEW
Mission statement: The University of Washington Libraries ResearchWorks Service provides faculty, researchers, and students tools to archive and/or publish the products of research, including datasets, monographs, images, journal articles, and technical reports.

Year publishing activities began: 1998

Organization: services are distributed across library units/departments

Total FTE in support of publishing activities: professional staff (1.5); graduate students (0.25)

Funding sources (%): library operating budget (100)

PUBLISHING ACTIVITIES
Library publications in 2015: campus-based faculty-driven journals (2); journals produced under contract/MOU for external groups (1); newsletters (1); ETDs (1,200); undergraduate capstones/honors theses (30)

Media formats: text; images; audio; video; data; concept maps, modeling, maps, or other visualizations

Disciplinary specialties: information studies; anthropology; fisheries; Southeast Asia

Top publications: ETDs; *Journal of Indo-Pacific Archaeology* (journal); *Advances in Classification Research Online* (journal); *Slovene Studies Journal* (journal); Jackson School of International Studies task force reports

Percentage of journals that are peer reviewed: 0

Internal partners: campus departments or programs; individual faculty; graduate students; undergraduate students

External partners: The Society for Slovene Studies; ASIS&T SIG/CR

Publishing platform(s): CONTENTdm; DSpace; OJS

Digital preservation strategy: ArchiveIt; DPN; HathiTrust; LOCKSS; Portico

Additional services: graphic design (print or web); training; analytics; cataloging; metadata; ISSN registry; DOI assignment/allocation of identifiers; author copyright advisory; digitization; hosting of supplemental content

UNIVERSITY OF WATERLOO
University of Waterloo Library

Primary Unit: Digital Initiatives
LibDI@library.uwaterloo.ca

Primary Contact: Pascal Calarco
Associate University Librarian, Research & Digital Discovery Services
519-888-4567
pvcalarco@uwaterloo.ca

Website: www.lib.uwaterloo.ca

Social media: www.facebook.com/danaporterlibrary; @UWLibrary

PROGRAM OVERVIEW
Mission statement: The Library provides open access publishing services for faculty and students based on Open Journal Systems, DSpace, Islandora, and Dataverse platforms. We are a member of CrossRef, and can issue DOIs for hosted publications, and can offer DOIs to research data via DataCite Canada. We work individually with prospective editors and authors, and can also assist with ISSN registration and journal indexing referrals.

Year publishing activities began: 1998

Organization: services are distributed across library units/departments

Total FTE in support of publishing activities: professional staff (1.5); paraprofessional staff (.25); undergraduates (0.1)

Funding sources (%): library operating budget (100)

PUBLISHING ACTIVITIES
Library publications in 2015: campus-based faculty-driven journals (3); campus-based student-driven journals (2); journals produced under contract/MOU for external groups (3); newsletters (6); databases (1); ETDs (979)

Media formats: text; images; data

Disciplinary specialties: disability studies; food science; sociology and criminology; mechanical engineering; geography

Top publications: ENGINE: Pre-Print Server for IEEE Society for Vehicular Technology (preprints); *Canadian Journal of Disability Studies* (journal); *Canadian Graduate Journal of Sociology and Criminology* (journal); *Canadian Journal of Food Safety* (journal)

Percentage of journals that are peer reviewed: 80

Internal partners: campus departments or programs; individual faculty; graduate students; undergraduate students

External partners: Canadian Disability Studies Association-Association Canadienne des Études sur l'Incapacité; Theses Canada; Canadian Association of Food Safety

Publishing platform(s): DSpace; Fedora; Islandora; OJS; Dataverse

Digital preservation strategy: Scholars Portal; digital preservation services under discussion

Additional services: outreach; training; analytics; cataloging; metadata; notification of A&I sources; ISSN registry; ISBN registry; DOI assignment/allocation of identifiers; open URL support; dataset management; contract/license preparation; author copyright advisory; digitization; hosting of supplemental content

ADDITIONAL INFORMATION

Plans for expansion/future directions: We're expanding our ETD repository to include faculty and student scholarship this year. As open access monograph publishing expands, we are tracking OMS and may implement if warranted. We will be expanding research data management activities as well.

UNIVERSITY OF WISCONSIN-MILWAUKEE
University of Wisconsin-Milwaukee Libraries

Primary Unit: User Services
open-access@uwm.edu

Primary Contact: Tim Gritten
Assistant Director of Libraries for User Services
414-229-6200
gritten@uwm.edu

Website: dc.uwm.edu

PROGRAM OVERVIEW
Mission statement: UWM Digital Commons, a service of the University of Wisconsin-Milwaukee Libraries, is a virtual showcase for UWM's research and creative profiles. Members of the UWM academic community are encouraged to contribute any completed scholarship for long-term preservation and worldwide electronic accessibility.

Year publishing activities began: 2012

Organization: services are distributed across library units/departments

Total FTE in support of publishing activities: professional staff (2); graduate students (0.5)

Funding sources (%): library operating budget

PUBLISHING ACTIVITIES
Library publications in 2015: campus-based faculty-driven journals (1); monographs (3); textbooks (1); technical/research reports (4); student conference papers and proceedings (3); ETDs (510)

Media formats: text; images; video; data; concept maps, modeling, maps, or other visualizations

Disciplinary specialties: geology; geography; architecture; urban planning; library science

Top publications: *International Journal of Geospatial and Environmental Research* (journal); *Cell and Molecular Biology: What We Know & How We Found Out* (monograph); "Searching the Archive of Our Own: The Usefulness of the Tagging

197

Structure" (thesis or dissertation); *The Small Public Library: Design Guide, Site Selection, and Design Case Study* (monograph); "The Zen of Web Discovery" (scholarly article)

Percentage of journals that are peer reviewed: 100

Internal partners: campus departments or programs; individual faculty; graduate students; undergraduate students

Publishing platform(s): bepress (Digital Commons)

Digital preservation strategy: digital preservation services under discussion

Additional services: copyediting; training; cataloging; metadata; ISBN registry; business model development; author copyright advisory; other author advisory; digitization; hosting of supplemental content

ADDITIONAL INFORMATION

Plans for expansion/future directions: DOI assignment; audio/video streaming

VALPARAISO UNIVERSITY
Christopher Center for Library and Information Resources

Primary Unit: Library Services

Primary Contact: Jonathan Bull
Scholarly Communication Services Librarian
219-464-5771
jon.bull@valpo.edu

Website: scholar.valpo.edu

PROGRAM OVERVIEW
Mission statement: ValpoScholar, a service of the Christopher Center Library and the Valparaiso University Law Library, is a digital repository and publication platform designed to collect, preserve, and make accessible the academic output of Valpo faculty, students, staff, and affiliates.

Year publishing activities began: 2011

Organization: services are distributed across library units/departments

Total FTE in support of publishing activities: professional staff (1); paraprofessional staff (0.5); graduate students (0.25); undergraduate students (0.25)

Funding sources (%): library materials budget (10); library operating budget (70); endowment income (20)

PUBLISHING ACTIVITIES
Library publications in 2015: campus-based faculty-driven journals (6); campus-based student-driven journals (3); monographs (1); textbooks (1); technical/research reports (6); faculty scholarship (1000); student scholarship (450); newsletters (5); ETDs (55); curricular maps (OERs)

Media formats: text; images; audio; video; data; concept maps, modeling, maps, or other visualizations

Disciplinary specialties: law; business; liberal arts; creative writing (fiction)

Top publications: *Valparaiso University Law Review* (journal); *The Journal of Values-Based Leadership* (journal); *Third World Legal Studies* (journal); *Valparaiso Fiction Review* (journal); *The Valpo CORE Reader* (journal)

Percentage of journals that are peer reviewed: 40

Internal partners: campus departments or programs; individual faculty; graduate students; undergraduate students

Publishing platform(s): bepress (Digital Commons); CONTENTdm; SelectedWorks

Digital preservation strategy: CLOCKSS; LOCKSS; in-house; digital preservation services under discussion

Additional services: print-on-demand; typesetting; training; analytics; cataloging; metadata ISSN registry; open URL support; peer review management; author copyright advisory; other author advisory; digitization; image services; hosting of supplemental content

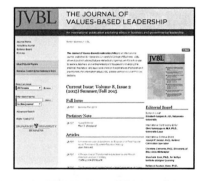

HIGHLIGHTED PUBLICATION

JVBL strives to publish articles that are intellectually rigorous yet of practical use to leaders, teachers, and entrepreneurs and focuses on converging the practical, theoretical, and applicable ideas and experiences of scholars and practitioners.

scholar.valpo.edu/jvbl

VANDERBILT UNIVERSITY
Jean and Alexander Heard Library

Primary Unit: Scholarly Communications

Primary Contact: Clifford B. Anderson
Director, Scholarly Communications
615-322-6938
clifford.anderson@vanderbilt.edu

Website: library.vanderbilt.edu/scholarly

Social media: @vandylibraries

PROGRAM OVERVIEW
Mission statement: The Jean and Alexander Heard Library fosters emerging modes of open access publishing by providing scholarly, technical, and financial support for the digital dissemination of faculty, student, and staff publications. The library maintains several publishing initiatives through its scholarly communication program. Currently, it publishes four peer-reviewed, open access journals—*AmeriQuests, Homiletic, Vanderbilt e-Journal of Luso-Hispanic Studies,* and the *Vanderbilt Undergraduate Research Journal*—using Open Journal Systems software. It also hosts a database of electronic theses and dissertations in cooperation with the Graduate School. Additionally, the library distributes undergraduate capstone projects through its institutional repository.

Year publishing activities began: 2004

Organization: services are distributed across library units/departments

Total FTE in support of publishing activities: professional staff (2)

Funding sources (%): library operating budget (100)

PUBLISHING ACTIVITIES
Library publications in 2015: campus-based faculty-driven journals (3); campus-based student-driven journals (1); ETDs (410); undergraduate capstones/honors theses (45)

Media formats: text; images

Disciplinary specialties: American studies; homiletics; Luso-Hispanic studies

Top publications: *AmeriQuests* (journal); *Homiletic* (journal); *Vanderbilt e-Journal of Luso-Hispanic Studies* (journal); *Vanderbilt Undergraduate Research Journal* (journal)

Percentage of journals that are peer reviewed: 100

Internal partners: campus departments or programs; individual faculty; graduate students; undergraduate students

External partners: Academy of Homiletics

Publishing platform(s): DSpace; OJS; ETD-db

Digital preservation strategy: LOCKSS; in-house

Additional services: outreach; training; cataloging; metadata; DOI assignment/ allocation of identifiers; author copyright advisory

VILLANOVA UNIVERSITY
Falvey Memorial Library

Primary Unit: Falvey Memorial Library

Primary Contact: Darren Poley
Scholarly Outreach Librarian & Team Leader
610-519-6371
darren.poley@villanova.edu

Website: journals.villanova.edu

PROGRAM OVERVIEW
Mission statement: In support of Villanova University's academic mission, the library is committed to the creation and dissemination of scholarship; utilizing digital modes and exploring new media for scholarly communication; and whenever possible, fostering open and public access to the intellectual contributions it publishes.

Year publishing activities began: 2009

Organization: services are distributed across library units/departments

Total FTE in support of publishing activities: professional staff (1.5)

Funding sources (%): library operating budget (100)

PUBLISHING ACTIVITIES
Library publications in 2015: campus-based faculty-driven journals (3); journals produced under contract/MOU for external groups (2); student conference papers and proceedings (1)

Media formats: text; images

Disciplinary specialties: American Catholic studies; Catholic higher education; theatre; humanities; liberal arts and sciences

Top publications: *Journal of Catholic Higher Education* (journal); *American Catholic Studies* (journal); *Expositions* (journal); *Concept* (journal); *Praxis* (journal)

Percentage of journals that are peer reviewed: 100

Internal partners: campus departments or programs; individual faculty; graduate students

External partners: American Catholic Historical Society; Association of Catholic Colleges and Universities

Publishing platform(s): OJS

Digital preservation strategy: in-house

Additional services: graphic design (print or web); outreach; training; analytics; metadata; digitization

ADDITIONAL INFORMATION
Plans for expansion/future directions: Continued cultivation of on-campus partnerships with the goal of developing and launching new faculty-driven, peer-reviewed journal projects in a variety of disciplines.

HIGHLIGHTED PUBLICATION

Expositions is an online journal where scholars from multiple disciplines gather as colleagues to converse about common texts and questions in the humanities.

expositions.journals.villanova.edu

VIRGINIA COMMONWEALTH UNIVERSITY
VCU Libraries

Primary Unit: Digital Technologies

Primary Contact: Sam Byrd
Digital Collections Systems Librarian
804-827-3556
sbyrd2@vcu.edu

Website: scholarscompass.vcu.edu

PROGRAM OVERVIEW
Mission statement: Scholars Compass is a publishing platform for the intellectual output of VCU's academic, research, and administrative communities. Its goal is to provide wide and stable access to the exemplary work of VCU's faculty, researchers, students, and staff. VCU Libraries administers and oversees the Scholars Compass.

Year publishing activities began: 2003

Organization: centralized library publishing unit/department

Total FTE in support of publishing activities: professional staff (0.3)

Funding sources (%): library operating budget (100)

PUBLISHING ACTIVITIES
Library publications in 2015: journals produced under contract/MOU for external groups (1); ETDs (538); undergraduate capstones/honors theses (137)

Media formats: text; images; audio; video; data; concept maps, modeling, maps, or other visualizations; multimedia/interactive content

Disciplinary specialties: art and design; psychology; medical sciences; theatre and performance studies; public health

Top publications: *Journal of Social Theory in Art Education* (journal); *British Virginia* (blog/journal); "Story-Telling Through the Design of a Permanent Mission Trip Training and Housing Facility" (thesis or dissertation); "Emancipators, Protectors, and Anomalies: Free Black Slaveowners in Virginia" (article); "Remembering through Music: Music Therapy and Dementia" (article)

Percentage of journals that are peer reviewed: 100

Internal partners: campus departments or programs; individual faculty; graduate students; undergraduate students

External partners: Caucus of Social Theory in Art Education (CSTAE)

Publishing platform(s): bepress (Digital Commons)

Digital preservation strategy: in-house; digital preservation services under discussion

Additional services: marketing; outreach; training; cataloging; metadata author copyright advisory; other author advisory; digitization hosting of supplemental content; audio/video streaming

ADDITIONAL INFORMATION

Plans for expansion/future directions: We plan to host journals and conference proceedings, in addition to publishing scholarly articles and monographs.

VIRGINIA TECH
University Libraries

Primary Unit: Scholarly Communication
gailmac@vt.edu

Primary Contact: Gail McMillan
Director, Scholarly Communication
540-231-9252
gailmac@vt.edu

Website: ejournals.lib.vt.edu; scholar.lib.vt.edu; econferences.lib.vt.edu

PROGRAM OVERVIEW
Mission statement: Virginia Tech's Libraries have put renewed emphasis on publishing, though we have hosted open access, peer-reviewed ejournals since 1989 and ETDs since 1996. We began offering Open Journal Systems (OJS) in 2012 and Open Conference Systems (OCS) in 2013. We are continuing to expand our publishing services and will support the many products of research and scholarship, including data visualization, interactive "books," and Open Education Resources. We are open to exploring faculty interests in publishing research and scholarship that is more than paper online, such as e-textbooks with interactive components and multimedia works. All collaborations result in sustainable publications that are included in our preservation strategy with the MetaArchive Cooperative. Like most library services, our publishing support is provided without charge and it is not limited to working with just the Virginia Tech community.

Year publishing activities began: 1989

Organization: centralized library publishing unit/department

Total FTE in support of publishing activities: professional staff (0.25); paraprofessional staff (1); undergraduate students (0.5)

Funding sources (%): library operating budget (100)

PUBLISHING ACTIVITIES
Library publications in 2015: campus-based faculty-driven journals (1); journals produced under contract/MOU for external groups (4); monographs (20); technical/research reports (57); faculty conference papers and proceedings (135); ETDs (2411)

Media formats: text; images; audio; video; data; concept maps, modeling, maps, or other visualizations; multimedia/interactive content; all/any format

Disciplinary specialties: technology education; Virginia Tech research; integrative STEM education; transportation studies

Top publications: Virginia Tech ETDs; *Journal of Technology Education* (journal); *ALAN Review* (journal); *Journal of Technology Studies* (journal); *Electronic Antiquity: Communicating the Classics* (journal)

Percentage of journals that are peer reviewed: 100

Internal partners: campus departments or programs (Virginia Tech Transportation Institute, Continuing and Professional Education); individual faculty

External partners: scholarly organizations (e.g., International Technology and Engineering Educators Association [ITEEA])

Publishing platform(s): OJS; OCS; DSpace; locally developed software

Digital preservation strategy: MetaArchive

Additional services: graphic design (print or web); training; analytics; cataloging; metadata; notification of A&I sources; ISSN registry; DOI assignment/allocation of identifiers; open URL support; dataset management; contract/license consultation; author copyright advisory; other author advisory; digitization; image services; data visualization; hosting of supplemental content; audio/video streaming

---

HIGHLIGHTED PUBLICATION

SPECTRA   THE ASPECT JOURNAL

Social, Political, Ethical, and Cultural Theory Archives (SPECTRA) is a student-led online scholarly journal that features work of an interdisciplinary nature and showcases research, explores controversial topics, and takes intellectual risks. SPECTRA includes works that operate within a problem-centered, theory-driven framework.

spectrajournal.org

ADDITIONAL INFORMATION

Plans for expansion/future directions: Virginia Tech Libraries' goal is to expand its publishing services to meet the needs of our university community. We are expanding our offerings through OJS and OCS, and we are anxious to publish Open Educational Resources, multimedia, interactive publications, data visualization, and so forth.

WAKE FOREST UNIVERSITY
Z. Smith Reynolds Library

Primary Unit: Library Partners Press
librarypartnerspress@wfu.edu

Primary Contact: William Kane
Director, Digital Publishing
336-758-6181
kanewp@wfu.edu

Website: digitalpublishing.wfu.edu

Social media: @WFUdigpub

PROGRAM OVERVIEW

Mission statement: Digital Publishing at Wake Forest University helps faculty, staff, and students create, collect, and convert otherwise unpublished works into digitally distributed books, journals, articles, and the like.

Year publishing activities began: 2011

Organization: services are distributed across campus

Total FTE in support of publishing activities: professional staff (1); paraprofessional staff (0.25)

Funding sources (%): library operating budget (75); non-library campus budget (25)

PUBLISHING ACTIVITIES

Library publications in 2015: monographs (10); textbooks (3); technical/research reports (6); faculty conference papers and proceedings (6); student conference papers and proceedings (6); newsletters (2); ETDs (50); undergraduate capstones/honors theses (25)

Media formats: text; images; audio; video; data; concept maps, modeling, maps, or other visualizations; multimedia/interactive content

Percentage of journals that are peer reviewed: 50

Internal partners: campus departments or programs; individual faculty; graduate students; undergraduate students

University press partners: Wake Forest University Press

Publishing platform(s): DSpace; Scalar; WordPress; locally developed software; Tizra; Biblioboard

Digital preservation strategy: Amazon Glacier; Amazon S3; Archive-It; HathiTrust; in-house; digital preservation services under discussion

Additional services: graphic design (print or web); print-on-demand; copy-editing; marketing; outreach; analytics; cataloging; metadata; compiling indexes and/or TOCs; ISBN registry; applying for Cataloging-in-Publication Data; DOI assignment/allocation of identifiers; business model development; budget preparation; contract/license preparation; author copyright advisory; other author advisory; digitization; audio/video streaming

ADDITIONAL INFORMATION
Plans for expansion/future directions: Moving toward offering print-on-demand services.

WASHINGTON UNIVERSITY IN ST. LOUIS
University Libraries

Primary Unit: Scholarly Publishing
digital@wumail.wustl.edu

Primary Contact: Emily Symonds Stenberg
Digital Publishing and Preservation Librarian
314-935-8329
emily.stenberg@wustl.edu

Website: openscholarship.wustl.edu

Social media: @digitalwustl

PROGRAM OVERVIEW

Mission statement: The mission of the Washington University in St. Louis publishing program is to provide alternatives to traditional publishing avenues and to promote and disseminate original scholarly works of the university community. Publishing is supported through two independent library repositories on the main and medical campuses: Open Scholarship provides a platform for the university community to make their scholarly and creative works available, providing free and open access whenever possible. The Scholarly Publishing department of the University Libraries provides overall administration for the repository, while the Law Library, recently merged with University Libraries, supports and manages publications affiliated with the School of Law. DigitalCommons@Becker enhances the visibility of scholarly work created through the School of Medicine, including faculty research and graduate capstones.

Year publishing activities began: 2009

Organization: centralized library publishing unit/department

Total FTE in support of publishing activities: professional staff (1.7); graduate students (0.8)

Funding sources (%): library operating budget (80); endowment income (20)

PUBLISHING ACTIVITIES

Library publications in 2015: campus-based faculty-driven journals (1); campus-based student-driven journals (4); monographs (3); ETDs (320); undergraduate capstones/honors theses (28); technical reports (494); graduate independent studies/capstones (18); faculty-driven digital projects

Media formats: text; images; audio; video

Disciplinary specialties: audiology and communication sciences; engineering; human research protection; law; social work and public health

Top publications: *Washington University Journal of American Indian & Alaska Native Health* (journal); *Washington University Law Review* (journal); *Transition to Higher Mathematics: Structure and Proof (Second Edition)* (OER); "Edith Wharton: Vision and Perception in Her Short Stories" (thesis or dissertation); "Statistical Trends in the Journal of the American Medical Association and Implications for Training Across the Continuum of Medical Education" (scholarly article)

Percentage of journals that are peer reviewed: 20

Internal partners: campus departments or programs; individual faculty; graduate students; undergraduate students

Publishing platform(s): bepress (Digital Commons)

Digital preservation strategy: in-house

Additional services: graphic design (print or web); copy-editing; marketing; cataloging; metadata; ISBN registry; DOI assignment/allocation of identifiers; dataset management; contract/license preparation; author copyright advisory; other author advisory; digitization; ORCID assignment for authors

ADDITIONAL INFORMATION

Additional information: For information about Law School publications, contact Dorie Bertram, bertram@wustl.edu. For information about DigitalCommons@ Becker, contact Amy Suiter, suitera@wustm.wustl.edu.

Plans for expansion/future directions: Expanding online journal and monograph offerings.

WAYNE STATE UNIVERSITY
Wayne State University Library System

Primary Unit: Digital Publishing
scholarscooperative@wayne.edu

Primary Contact: Joshua Neds-Fox
Coordinator for Digital Publishing
313-577-4460
jnf@wayne.edu

Website: scholarscooperative.wayne.edu

PROGRAM OVERVIEW
Mission statement: Wayne State's Digital Publishing Unit works to make unique, important, or institutionally relevant content available to the world at large.

Year publishing activities began: 2010

Organization: centralized library publishing unit/department

Total FTE in support of publishing activities: professional staff (3); paraprofessional staff (0.5)

Funding sources (%): library operating budget (100)

PUBLISHING ACTIVITIES
Library publications in 2015: campus-based faculty-driven journals (1); campus-based student-driven journals (1); ETDs (200); undergraduate capstones/honors theses (3)

Library-administered university press publications in 2015: journals produced under contract/MOU for external groups (13)

Media formats: text; images

Top publications: *Journal of Modern Applied Statistical Methods* (journal); *Clinical Research in Practice* (journal)

Percentage of journals that are peer reviewed: 80

Internal partners: campus departments or programs; individual faculty; graduate students; undergraduate students

University press partners: Wayne State University Press

Publishing platform(s): bepress (Digital Commons); Fedora; locally developed software

Digital preservation strategy: in-house

Additional services: graphic design (print or web); typesetting; outreach; training; analytics; metadata; author copyright advisory; digitization; hosting of supplemental content

---

HIGHLIGHTED PUBLICATION

Journal of
Modern Applied
Statistical Methods

Vol. 12, No. 1 • May 2013

JMASM is an independent, peer-reviewed, open access journal providing a scholarly outlet for applied (non)parametric statisticians, data analysts, researchers, psychometricians, quantitative or qualitative evaluators, and methodologists.

digitalcommons.wayne.edu/jmasm

WESTERN WASHINGTON UNIVERSITY
Western Libraries

Primary Unit: Scholarly Communication Unit
westerncedar@wwu.edu

Primary Contact: Jenny Oleen
Scholarly Communication Librarian
360-650-2613
jenny.oleen@wwu.edu

Website: cedar.wwu.edu

PROGRAM OVERVIEW
Mission statement: Western CEDAR collects, preserves, and globally disseminates digital copies of the intellectual output of Western Washington University.

Year publishing activities began: 2014

Organization: centralized library publishing unit/department

Total FTE in support of publishing activities: professional staff (1); paraprofessional staff (1)

Funding sources (%): library operating budget (100)

PUBLISHING ACTIVITIES
Library publications in 2015: ETDs (60); faculty conference proceedings (300); student conference proceedings (80)

Media formats: text; images; audio; video; data; concept maps, modeling, maps, or other visualizations

Internal partners: campus departments or programs; individual faculty; graduate students

Publishing platform(s): bepress (Digital Commons)

Digital preservation strategy: digital preservation services under discussion

Additional services: marketing; training; digitization

ADDITIONAL INFORMATION

Plans for expansion/future directions: Western CEDAR is in the planning process for publishing both a journal and a conference, with the intention of moving further in that direction in the future.

LIBRARIES OUTSIDE NORTH AMERICA

AUSTRALIAN NATIONAL UNIVERSITY
Australian National University Library

Primary Unit: Lorena Kanellopoulos
anupress@anu.edu.au

Primary Contact: Lorena Kanellopoulos
Manager ANU Press
+ 61 2 6125 4536
lorena.kanellopoulos@anu.edu.au

Website: press.anu.edu.au; anulib.anu.edu.au

Social media: @ANU_Press

PROGRAM OVERVIEW
Mission statement: ANU E Press, as it was originally known, was established in 2003 to explore and enable new modes of scholarly publishing. Taking advantage of new information and communication technologies to make available the intellectual output of the ANU academic community, ANU E Press was Australia's first primarily electronic academic publisher. After 10 years of production, in early 2014 ANU E Press changed its name to ANU Press to reflect the changes the publication industry had seen since 2003. Now digital publication has become the norm across publishing; the Press no longer needs to set itself apart as a digital publisher, and so has taken the traditional academic publishing name of ANU Press. The primary focus of ANU Press is the electronic production of scholarly works. All works are also available for purchase through a print-on-demand (PoD) service. ANU Press produces fully peer-reviewed research publications and is recognised by DIISRTE as a commercial publisher, enabling ANU Press authors to gain full recognition under the Higher Education Research Data Collection scheme.

Year publishing activities began: 2003

Organization: decentralised and centralised. Peer-review process decentralised to Editorial Boards across campus. Production process centralised in the Press.

Total FTE in support of publishing activities: professional staff (4.5)

Funding sources (%): library operating budget (80); sales revenue (20)

PUBLISHING ACTIVITIES
Library publications in 2015: campus-based faculty-driven journals (5); campus-based student-driven journals (3); monographs (60); textbooks (1); faculty conference papers and proceedings (47); ETDs (759)

Media formats: text; audio; video; multimedia/interactive content

Disciplinary specialties: humanities; social sciences; law; public policy; science

Top publications: *Black Words White Page* (book); *Security and Privacy* (book); *Interpreting Chekhov* (book); *Aboriginal History* (journal); *Public Policy* (book)

Percentage of journals that are peer reviewed: 100

Internal partners: campus departments or programs

Publishing platform(s): DSpace; WordPress

Digital preservation strategy: CLOCKSS; in-house; PANDORA-NLA

Additional services: graphic design (print or web); print-on-demand; typesetting; marketing; outreach; training; cataloging; metadata; ISSN registry; ISBN registry; applying for Cataloging-in-Publication Data; DOI assignment/allocation of identifiers peer review management; budget preparation; contract/license preparation; author copyright advisory; digitization; image services; hosting of supplemental content; audio/video streaming; quality control and proofreading

ADDITIONAL INFORMATION
Plans for expansion/future directions: The ANU Press has commenced publishing eTextbooks in 2014 and also will be merging the Digital Repository unit within the Press.

HIGHLIGHTED PUBLICATION

ANU Press launched their eTextbook series in 2014 with this title. This development represents a radical change in publishing aiming to bring text books for free to the world. *The Joy of Sanskrit* is a complete first-year course of twenty-five weeks designed for university students.

press.anu.edu.au/titles/anu-etext/the-joy-of-sanskrit

GEORG-AUGUST-UNIVERSITÄT GÖTTINGEN
State and University Library Göttingen

Primary Unit: Electronic Publishing

Primary Contact: Margo Bargheer
Head of Electronic Publishing
+ 49 551 399 1188
mbarghe@gwdg.de

Website: www.sub.uni-goettingen.de/en/electronic-publishing

PROGRAM OVERVIEW
Mission statement: The library provides open access-oriented publishing services to researchers, including Goettingen University Press, repositories for theses and peer-reviewed publications. In addition, a central open access fund has been established, which covers article processing charges and monitors the uptake of Gold Open Access at the University. These service areas are combined with strategic involvement in national and international initiatives, such as the Confederation of Open Access Repositories (COAR) and OpenAIRE, the European-wide open access infrastructure for publications. These institutional activities work in both directions; they are crucial for enhancing local services and vice versa feed experiences and lessons learned into international collaborations.

Year publishing activities began: 1996

Organization: centralized library publishing unit/department

Total FTE in support of publishing activities: professional staff (3); paraprofessional staff (2)

Funding sources (%): library materials budget (10); library operating budget (40); non-library campus budget (15); grants (5); sales revenue (15); licensing revenue (1); other (14)

PUBLISHING ACTIVITIES
Library publications in 2015: campus-based student-driven journals (1); monographs and annals (39); textbooks and exhibition catalogs (7); technical/research reports (10); faculty conference papers and proceedings (14); ETDs (600)

Media formats: text; audio; DVD

Disciplinary specialties: P2P communication in law sciences (proceedings, pre-legislation discourse); environmental history; ethics in medicine

Top publications: *Sex and Gender in Biomedicine* (monograph); *Wood Production, Wood Technology, and Biotechnological Impacts* (monograph); *Rechtliche Rahmenbedingungen von Open-Access-Publikationen* (monograph); *Mathematische Grundlagen in Biologie und Geowissenschaften* (textbook); *Poems at the Edge of Differences* (monograph)

Percentage of journals that are peer reviewed: 100

Internal partners: campus departments or programs; individual faculty; graduate students

External partners: information hub on Open Access (open-access.net); FADAF; NW-FVA; OAPEN; Akademie der Wissenschaften zu Göttingen; working group of German university presses; several German project partners that also run library publishing activities

Publishing platform(s): DSpace; locally developed software

Digital preservation strategy: in-house

Additional services: graphic design (print or web); print-on-demand; typesetting; copy-editing; marketing; outreach; training; analytics; cataloging; metadata; ISSN registry; ISBN registry; DOI assignment/allocation of identifiers; open URL support; dataset management; peer review management; business model development; budget preparation; contract/license preparation; author copyright advisory; other author advisory; digitization; image services; hosting of supplemental content; audio/video streaming

ADDITIONAL INFORMATION
Plans for expansion/future directions: Projects and infrastructure for research data management and virtual research environments are becoming a more important part of our service portfolio. We will work on bringing these activities into networked infrastructures.

MONASH UNIVERSITY
Monash University Library

Primary Unit: Research Infrastructure Division

Primary Contact: Andrew Harrison
Research Repository Librarian
+ 61 3 9905 2682
andrew.harrison@monash.edu

Website: arrow.monash.edu.au

PROGRAM OVERVIEW
Mission statement: The Monash University Research Repository provides a place for the Monash research community to store and manage digital research data and related publications. The repository aims to promote Monash research by making it discoverable and accessible online for the worldwide research community. The repository contains accepted versions of published works like books, book chapters, journal articles, and conference papers. Non-published manuscripts and gray literature like theses, technical reports, working and discussion papers, and conference posters are collected. Research data holdings, datasets, image collections, audio, and video files also are included in the repository.

Year publishing activities began: 2006

Organization: centralized library publishing unit/department

Total FTE in support of publishing activities: professional staff (1.5); paraprofessional staff (3)

Funding sources (%): library operating budget (100)

PUBLISHING ACTIVITIES
Library publications in 2015: campus-based faculty-driven journals (7); ETDs (892)

Library-administered university press publications in 2015: 25 monographs

Media formats: text; images; audio; video; data

Disciplinary specialties: poetry; prose; environmental crisis; Geographic Information Systems; environmental data

Top publications: *Philosophy Activism Nature* (journal); *Applied GIS* (journal)

Percentage of journals that are peer reviewed: 100

Internal partners: campus departments or programs; graduate students

Publishing platform(s): VITAL

Digital preservation strategy: digital preservation services under review

Additional services: cataloging; metadata; DOI assignment/allocation of identifiers; hosting of supplemental content

ADDITIONAL INFORMATION

Plans for expansion/future directions: Implementing new software to replace existing repository software to allow easier self-submission of research data as primary focus of the library's efforts. Publications will be handed back to the university research office and the new system will integrate with a new current research information system (CRIS) to allow automated dissemination of publication data. Theses publication will be automated within the Graduate School for the collection of digital-only theses manuscripts and published automatically into the new library system.

STOCKHOLM UNIVERSITY
Stockholm University Library

Primary Unit: Communications Department
publish@su.se

Primary Contact: Birgitta Hellmark Lindgren (PhD)
Head of Communications and Deputy Library Director
+ 46 7 0190 7769
birgitta.hellmark-lindgren@sub.su.se

Website: stockholmuniversitypress.se

Social media: facebook.com/stockholmuniversitypress; @SthlmUniPress; linkedin.com/company/stockholm-university-press; blog.stockholmuniversitypress.se

PROGRAM OVERVIEW
Mission statement: Stockholm University Press is a publicly financed operation with its main goal to provide public access to peer-reviewed scientific results in multiple formats, both nationally and internationally. The Press provides access to electronic journals and books free of charge, and to printed books at cost prices. We aim to make journals and books affordable, and to give them the widest possible dissemination so that researchers around the world can find and access the information they need without barriers. SUP was founded after a decision made by the Vice Chancellor in December 2012.

Year publishing activities began: 2014

Organization: services are distributed across library units/departments

Total FTE in support of publishing activities: professional staff (2.5)

Funding sources (%): library operating budget and APC and BPC

PUBLISHING ACTIVITIES
Library publications in 2015: campus-based faculty-driven journals (3)

Library-administered university press publications in 2015: monographs (3); articles in the journal *Rural Landscapes*

Media formats: text; images; data; concept maps; modeling, maps; or other visualizations

Disciplinary specialties: humanities; science; social sciences; law

Top publications: *Rural Landscapes: Society, Environment, History* (journal); *Platonic Occasions* (book); *From Clerks to Copora* (book); *Festival Romanistica* (book)

Percentage of journals that are peer reviewed: 100

Internal partners: campus departments or programs

Publishing platform(s): OJS; Rua

Digital preservation strategy: DiVA (Digitala Vetenskapliga Arkivet)

Additional services: graphic design (print or web); print-on-demand; typesetting; copy-editing; marketing; outreach; analytics; cataloging; metadata; ISSN registry; ISBN registry; dataset management; peer review management; business model development; contract/license preparation; author copyright advisory; other author advisory; image services; data visualization

ADDITIONAL INFORMATION

Plans for expansion/future directions: From autumn 2014 the Stockholm University Library offers a new dissertation support open to all doctoral students at Stockholm University. The idea is to simplify the publishing process. In conjunction with the electronic posting, the doctoral students may choose to get help with the production, distribution, and marketing of their dissertations. We also will have a publishing service for "gray area literature," which will offer a limited support similar to that of the press.

SWINBURNE UNIVERSITY OF TECHNOLOGY
Swinburne Library

Primary Unit: Information Resources

Primary Contact: Nyssa Parkes
Content Management Librarian
nparkes@swinburne.edu.au

Website: www.swinburne.edu.au/library/services-researchers/build-your
-research-profile/publish-online-journal; commons.swinburne.edu.au

PROGRAM OVERVIEW
Mission statement: The Swinburne Online Journals service provides publishing support to Swinburne faculties and research centres who publish online open access journals. We provide hosting software and technical assistance as well as help and advice on general online publishing and copyright issues. Swinburne Commons is the centralised service for the management and distribution of digital media content produced across Swinburne. The Commons draws together quality digital media content from across the University to highlight the research strengths, teaching excellence, student accomplishments, and unique aspects of Swinburne.

Year publishing activities began: 2006

Organization: services are distributed across library units/departments

Total FTE in support of publishing activities: professional staff (3)

PUBLISHING ACTIVITIES
Library publications in 2015: campus-based faculty-driven journals (3); video and audio publishing; videos created at the university are disseminated centrally through the library's service.

Media formats: text; images; audio; video

Disciplinary specialties: mathematics (videos); psychology (journal); business (journal)

Top publications: *Sensoria: A Journal of Mind, Brain, and Culture* (journal); *Journal of Contemporary Issues in Business and Government* (journal)

Percentage of journals that are peer reviewed: 100

Internal partners: individual faculty

Publishing platform(s): OJS; Equella/Kaltura

Digital preservation strategy: digital preservation services under discussion with National Library of Australia

Additional services: training; analytics; metadata; ISSN registry; DOI assignment/allocation of identifiers; contract/license preparation; hosting of supplemental content; audio/video streaming

UNIVERSITY OF CRAIOVA, ROMANIA
Alexandru and Aristia Aman Dolj County Library

Primary Unit: Media Department
presa@aman.ro

Primary Contact: Lucian Dindirica
+ 40 7 2222 0606
lucian.dindirica@yahoo.com

Social media: facebook.com/bibliotecajudeteana.aman.ro

PROGRAM OVERVIEW
Mission statement: The main objective of our publishing activities is to promote the results of academic research in various fields such as archeology; history (ancient, middle, modern and contemporary); theology; diplomacy; cultural studies; international relations; and European studies. Its purpose is also to establish a dialogue between different approaches to scholarship, by reuniting not only theoreticians, researchers, and analysts, but also individuals actively involved in the transformations in the international scene. We also support the editing and promotion of numerous works (poetry, prose) of local authors.

Year publishing activities began: 2009

Organization: centralized library publishing unit/department

Total FTE in support of publishing activities: professional staff (2.5)

Funding sources (%): library materials budget (60); library operating budget (30)

PUBLISHING ACTIVITIES
Library publications in 2015: campus-based faculty-driven journals (1); journals produced under contract/MOU for external groups (1); monographs (5); textbooks (30); technical/research reports (4); newsletters (12)

Media formats: text; data

Disciplinary specialties: history; diplomacy; cultural studies; theology; European studies

Top publications: *State and Society in Europe* (conference proceedings); *Journal of Humanities, Culture and Socila Sciences* (journal); Romanians in the History of Europe

Percentage of journals that are peer reviewed: 100

External partners: Cetatea de Scaun Publishing House, University of Craiova

Publishing platform(s): WordPress

Digital preservation strategy: academia.edu; Citefactor; SCIPIO

Additional services: graphic design (print or web); copy-editing; cataloging; ISSN registry; ISBN registry; applying for Cataloging-in-Publication Data; open URL support; peer review management; author copyright advisory; digitization; hosting of supplemental content

ADDITIONAL INFORMATION

Additional information: Alexandru and Aristia Aman Dolj County Library publishes or supports the publishing efforts for a large number of papers, covering a large area of topics and themes.

Plans for expansion/future directions: We have in plan the continuation of publishing activities, mainly of scientific journals and volumes signed by local authors. In this regard, we rely on the partnerships with Cetatea de Scaun Publishing House and Mitropolia Oltenia Publishing House.

UNIVERSITY OF HUDDERSFIELD
University of Huddersfield Computing and Library Services

Primary Unit: Information Resources
university.press@hud.ac.uk

Primary Contact: Graham Stone
Information Resources Manager
+ 44 (0) 148 447 2042
g.stone@hud.ac.uk

Website: unipress.hud.ac.uk

PROGRAM OVERVIEW
Mission statement: The University of Huddersfield Press publishes books, journals, and sound recordings. It provides an outlet for publication for University authors, to encourage new and aspiring authors to publish in their areas of subject expertise, and to raise the profile of the University through the Press publications. The principles governing the University of Huddersfield Press are that (i) all material published should be of high quality and peer reviewed; (ii) as a general rule, material should be published open access via the University Repository, in order to maximize the potential for dissemination to as wide an audience as possible (publications may also be made available by print-on-demand); and (iii) the Press will operate on a cost-recovery profit-sharing model, with any profits being reinvested into the Press.

Year publishing activities began: 2010

Organization: centralized library publishing unit/department

Total FTE in support of publishing activities: professional staff (1); paraprofessional staff (0.5)

Funding sources (%): library operating budget (15); non-library campus budget (55); grants (15); sales revenue (15)

PUBLISHING ACTIVITIES
Library publications in 2015: campus-based faculty-driven journals (7); monographs (2)

Library-administered university press publications in 2015: journals (4)

Media formats: text; images; audio; video; multimedia/interactive content; music CDs and downloads

Disciplinary specialties: history; music; education; art and design; performance magic

Top publications: *Huddersfield's Roll of Honour: 1914–1922* (monograph); *Noise In and as Music* (monograph); *Fields: Journal of Huddersfield Student Research* (journal); *Identity Papers* (journal); *Teaching in Lifelong Learning: A Journal to Inform and Improve Practice* (journal)

Percentage of journals that are peer reviewed: 85

Internal partners: campus departments or programs; individual faculty; graduate students

Publishing platform(s): EPrints; NMC Recordings for digital music downloads and CDs

Digital preservation strategy: Portico

Additional services: graphic design (print or web); marketing; outreach; training; analytics; ISSN registry; ISBN registry; DOI assignment/allocation of identifiers; business model development; budget preparation; contract/license preparation; author copyright advisory; other author advisory; hosting supplemental content; audio/video streaming

ADDITIONAL INFORMATION

Additional information: We now have two journals listed in DOAJ: *Teaching in Lifelong Learning* and *Journal of Performance Magic*. We will submit a further two in 2016. In addition, we also have our open access monographs listed in DOAB.

Plans for expansion/future directions: We plan to publish a further journal title in 2015–2016, and have a number of other titles in development. We also have a number of monographs and CDs in preparation for 2016.

UNIVERSITY OF MANCHESTER
University of Manchester Library

Primary Unit: Research Services
uml.scholarlycommunication@manchester.ac.uk

Primary Contact: Helen Dobson
+ 44 0 1612 758729
helen.j.dobson@manchester.ac.uk

PROGRAM OVERVIEW
Mission statement: The University of Manchester Library's publishing program has been developed to support the creation, dissemination, and preservation of knowledge. Our mission is to (i) sustain and enhance the research reputations of individuals and organizations affiliated with the University of Manchester; (ii) enhance the global research community's ability to access the University of Manchester's research outputs and Special Collections; and (iii) produce high-quality learning objects to support academic and personal development. Current publishing activities cover a range of materials, with an emphasis on open access content: (i) PhD theses and dissertations, technical reports and conference papers are published through the institutional repository, Manchester eScholar; (ii) learning objects are shared via JORUM; and (iii) image collections are made available via Luna Insight. The Library works in partnership with Manchester University Press to support the development of new journals.

Year publishing activities began: 2009

Organization: services are distributed across campus

Total FTE in support of publishing activities: professional staff (2); paraprofessional staff (4)

Funding sources (%): library operating budget (80); library materials budget (5); grants (5); sales revenue (5); charge backs (5)

PUBLISHING ACTIVITIES
Library publications in 2015: technical/research reports (129); ETDs (598); data objects; learning objects; digital images

Media formats: text; images; data; multimedia/interactive content

Disciplinary specialties: arts and humanities; social sciences; medical and human sciences; life sciences; physical and engineering sciences

Internal partners: individual faculty; campus departments or programs

University press partners: Manchester University Press

Publishing platform(s): Fedora

Digital preservation strategy: in-house

Additional services: marketing; outreach; training; analytics; cataloging; metadata; ISBN registry; DOI assignment/allocation of identifiers; dataset management; author copyright advisory; other author advisory; digitization; image services; hosting of supplemental content

ADDITIONAL INFORMATION

Plans for expansion/future directions: The Library is keen to develop new services and enhance existing services with new technologies to continue to meet the needs and expectations of the University of Manchester and the wider research community. The Library works in partnership with Manchester University Press, supporting new journals and investigating the demand for student-led open access journals. Titles due to launch in 2015–2016 include *James Baldwin Review* and a student-led medical journal.

UNIVERSITY OF TECHNOLOGY, SYDNEY
UTS Library

Primary Unit: UTSeScholarship
utsepress@uts.edu.au

Primary Contact: Julie-Anne Marshall
Manager, eResearch
+ 61 2 9514 4098
julie-anne.marshall@uts.edu.au

Website: epress.lib.uts.edu.au

Social media: @UTSePRESS; facebook.com/UTSePRESS; uts-epress.tumblr.com

PROGRAM OVERVIEW

Mission statement: UTS ePRESS is the digital, open access scholarly publishing arm of UTS. We publish high-quality scholarly titles across a wide range of academic disciplines, including governance, history, law, literacy, international studies, society and social justice, and indigenous studies. Focusing on open access digital formats only, UTS ePRESS currently publishes journals, books, and conference proceedings, and is the leading publisher of peer reviewed open access journals in Australasia. UTS ePRESS seeks to publish peer reviewed, scholarly literature in areas of strategic priority for UTS and beyond, attracting the involvement of leading scholars from around the world. In doing so, our aim is to enhance scholarly publishing by exploring, innovating, and enabling new modes of publication in the digital arena. UTS ePRESS is a not-for-profit publisher. We strongly support the free dissemination of scholarly material and, since our inception, have deepened our commitment to open access publishing, despite the growth of complex and diverse publishing models across the world. Our goal is to unlock publicly funded research and share knowledge that will benefit scholars, researchers, readers, and the public, and to extend its reach and impact by making it openly available and widely accessible to a global audience.

Year publishing activities began: 2004

Organization: centralized library publishing unit/department

Total FTE in support of publishing activities: professional staff (3.8)

Funding sources (%): library operating budget (100)

PUBLISHING ACTIVITIES

Library publications in 2015: campus-based faculty-driven journals (9); campus-based student-driven journals (2); journals produced under contract/MOU for external groups (2); monographs (2); faculty conference papers and proceedings (1); ceased journal titles available via open access (7)

Library-administered university press publications in 2015: As above. UTS ePRESS is the university's open access scholarly press, administered by UTS Library. The UTS institutional repository, OPUS, is separate from UTS ePRESS, but also managed by UTS Library.

Media formats: text; images; multimedia/interactive content

Disciplinary specialties: cultural studies; built environment; history and society; law and public administration; literacy

Percentage of journals that are peer reviewed: 100

Internal partners: individual faculty

Publishing platform(s): DSpace; OJS; OCS; Drupal

Digital preservation strategy: CLOCKSS; Portico

Additional services: graphic design (print or web); print-on-demand marketing; training; analytics; metadata; notification of A&I sources; ISSN registry; ISBN registry; applying for Cataloging-in-Publication Data; DOI assignment/allocation of identifiers; contract/license preparation; author copyright advisory; other author advisory; digitization; plagiarism detection service; DOI sourcing; format conversion (html); DOI registration

ADDITIONAL INFORMATION

Plans for expansion/future directions: UTS ePRESS will continue to implement strategies to consolidate our open access credentials and to enhance maximum accessibility, use, and reuse of our scholarly material while continuing to innovate in order to ensure we remain at the forefront of open access publishing.

UWE BRISTOL
Frenchay Library

Primary Unit: Research and Knowledge Exchange

Primary Contact: Anna Lawson
+ 01 1 7328 6438
anna.lawson@uwe.ac.uk

PROGRAM OVERVIEW
Mission statement: Through publishing work on the UWE Research Repository, we aim to provide immediate, worldwide open access to UWE research output that has previously been hidden or invisible outside of the university.

Year publishing activities began: 2010

Organization: centralized library publishing unit/department

Total FTE in support of publishing activities: professional staff (0.1); paraprofessional staff (0.25)

Funding sources (%): library operating budget (100)

PUBLISHING ACTIVITIES
Library publications in 2015: technical/research reports (12); faculty conference papers and proceedings (42); ETDs (23)

Media formats: text; images

Top publications: "Plenty More Fish in the Sea? A Working Paper on the Legal Issues Related to Fishing Beyond Maximum Sustainable Yield: A UK Case Study"; "The Interaction Between Equity and Credit Risks" (thesis or dissertation); "France at Reims: The Fourteenth Centenary of the Baptism of Clovis, 1896" (working paper); "From Zouaves Pontificaux to the Volontaires de l'Ouest: Catholic Volunteers and the French Nation, 1860-1910" (working paper); "Implementing the New Science of Risk Management to Tanker Freight Markets" (thesis or dissertation)

Internal partners: campus departments or programs; individual faculty; graduate students

Publishing platform(s): EPrints

Digital preservation strategy: no digital preservation services provided

Additional services: training; ISBN registry; author copyright advisory

LIBRARY PUBLISHING COALITION STRATEGIC AFFILIATES

Strategic Affiliates are entities (including service providers, library networks and consortia, non-profit organizations, and others) that share a common interest in this emerging field.

To become a Strategic Affiliate, contact the Library Publishing Coalition's Program Director, Sarah K. Lippincott (sarah@educopia.org).

ACRL
Association of Research Libraries (ARL)
bepress
BiblioLabs
Boston Library Consortium (BLC)
Coalition for Networked Information (CNI)
Council of Australian University Librarians (CAUL)
Digital Public Library of America (DPLA)
Five Colleges Librarians Council
HASTAC
Knowledge Unlatched
NASIG
OAN
OAPEN
Open Access Scholarly Publishers Association (OASPA)
Public Knowledge Project (PKP)
Reveal Digital
Scribe
SPARC
Society for Scholarly Publishing (SSP)
Tizra
Ubiquity Press
unglue.it
University of North Carolina Press

PLATFORMS, TOOLS, AND SERVICE PROVIDERS

Libraries work with a range of external software, tools, and service providers to support preservation, markup, conversion, hosting, allocation of identifiers, and other processes related to the publishing workflow. This following list compiles the names and websites of tools, software, and service providers employed by the libraries in this directory.

EDITORIAL/PRODUCTION

Amazon Createspace
www.createspace.com

Backstage Library Works
www.bslw.com

BookComp
www.bookcomp.com

Bookmasters
www.bookmasters.com

Calibre
www.calibre-ebook.com

Charlesworth
www.charlesworth-group.com

Data Conversion Laboratory, Inc.
www.dclab.com

Datapage
www.datapage.ie

Digital Library Systems Group
www.imageaccess.com/dlsg

epubli
www.epubli.co.uk

Hudson Microimaging
www.hudsonmicroimaging.com

Inera eXtyles
www.inera.com

Ingram Lightning Source
www.lightningsource.com

iThenthicate
www.ithenticate.com

Lulu
www.lulu.com

Media Preserve
www.themediapreserve.com

NewGen Knowledgeworks
www.newgen.co

Open Content Alliance
www.opencontentalliance.org

Oxygen
www.oxygenxml.com

Scene Savers
www.scenesavers.com

Sigil
www.github.com/user-none/Sigil

Spectrum Creative
www.spectrum-creative.com

Submittable
www.submittable.com

Texas Book Consortium
www.tamupress.com

TIPS Technical Publishing
www.technicalpublishing.com

Trigonix
www.trigonix.com/english

Ubiquity Press
www.ubiquitypress.com

UPNE
www.upne.com

Versioning Machine
www.v-machine.org

PLATFORM/HOSTING/INFRASTRUCTURE

@mire
www.atmire.com/website

Ambra
www.ambraproject.org

Artstor and Shared Shelf
www.artstor.org

bepress
www.bepress.com

Commons in a Box
www.commonsinabox.org

Connexions
www.cnx.org

CONTENTdm
www.contentdm.org

DataVerse
www.thedata.org

DigiTool by ExLibris
www.exlibrisgroup.com/category/
DigiToolOvervie

Django Web framework
www.djangoproject.com

DPubS
dpubs.org

Drupal
www.drupal.org

DSpace
www.dspace.org

Ensemble
www.ensemblevideo.com

EPrints
www.eprints.org/us

ETD-db
scholar.lib.vt.edu/ETD-db/index.shtml

XTF (eXtensible Text Framework)
xtf.cdlib.org

Fedora
www.fedora-commons.org

HUBzero
www.hubzero.org

Issuu
www.issuu.com

Kaltura
www.corp.kaltura.com

MediaAMP
www.mediaamp.org

MediaCAST
www.inventivetec.com

Omeka
www.omeka.org

OJS/OCS/OMP
pkp.sfu.ca/ojs
pkp.sfu.ca/ocs
pkp.sfu.ca/omp

Panopto
www.panopto.com

PressBooks
www.pressbooks.com

WordPress
www.wordpress.org

Scalar
scalar.usc.edu

Vimeo
www.vimeo.com

Soundcloud
www.soundcloud.com

VitalSource
www.vitalsource.com

Tizra
www.tizra.com

DISCOVERY/MARKETING

Altmetric.com
www.altmetric.com

EZID
www.n2t.net/ezid

bibapp
www.bibapp.org

LOC ISSN registry
www.loc.gov/issn

Bowker
www.bowker.com/en-US

MARCIVE
home.marcive.com

CrossRef
www.crossref.org

Plum Analytics
www.plumanalytics.com

DataCite
www.datacite.org

ProQuest
www.proquest.com

DOAJ
www.doaj.org

Serials Solutions
www.serialssolutions.com

EBSCO
www.ebscohost.com

DIGITAL PRESERVATION

ADPNet
www.adpnet.org

Archive-It
www.archive-it.org

Amazon Glacier
www.aws.amazon.com/glacier

Archivematica
www.archivematica.org

Amazon S3
www.aws.amazon.com/s3

Artefactual
www.artefactual.com

APTrust
www.aptrust.org

Chronopolis
chronopolis.sdsc.edu

CLOCKSS
www.clockss.org/clockss/Home

Dark Archive In The Sunshine State (DAITSS)
daitss.fcla.edu

Digital Preservation Network (DPN)
www.dpn.org

discoverygarden
www.discoverygarden.ca

DuraCloud
www.duracloud.org

HathiTrust
www.hathitrust.org

Hydra
www.projecthydra.org

Internet Archive
www.archive.org/index.php

Islandora
www.islandora.ca

LOCKSS
www.lockss.org

MetaArchive
www.metaarchive.org

Portico
www.portico.org/digital-preservation

Preservica
www.preservica.com

Rosetta
www.exlibrisgroup.com/category/
RosettaOverview

Safety Deposit Box
www.digital-preservation.com/
solution/safety-deposit-box

Scholars Portal
spotdocs.scholarsportal.info/display/sp/
home

Synergies
www.synergiescanada.org

UC3 Merritt
merritt.cdlib.org

CONSULTING

WorldShare Management Services
https://www.oclc.org/worldshare-
management-services.en.html

LIBRARY NETWORKS AND CONSORTIA

Networked Digital Library of Theses and Dissertations (NDLTD)
www.ndltd.org

Ontario Council of Research Libraries
www.ocul.on.ca

OhioLINK ETD Center
etd.ohiolink.edu

Texas Digital Library
www.tdl.org

Theses Canada
www.collectionscanada.gc.ca/
thesescanada/index-e.html

PERSONNEL INDEX

Agnew, Grace, 100
Anderson, Clifford B., 201
Bargheer, Margo, 221
Beatty, Joshua, 111
Beaubien, Sarah, x
Bernhardt, Beth, 168
Betz, Sonya, 121
Billings, Marilyn S., 149
Bjork, Karen, 93
Boczar, Jason, 184
Boock, Michael, 83
Buckland, Amy, 129
Bull, Jonathan, xi, 199
Byrd, Sam, 205
Calarco, Pascal, 195
Cohen, Jason, 154
Coleman, Jason, xi
Corbett, Hillary, xi, 77
Corbly, David, 172
Cornell, Deborah, 18
Coughlan, Rosarie, 98
Covey, Denise Troll, 10
Davis, Laura Drake, 60
Davis-Kahl, Stephanie, 52
De Groote, Sandy, 136
DeFelice, Barbara, 24
Deliyannides, Timothy S., 176
Dindirica, Lucian, 229
Dobson, Helen, 233
Dohe, Kate, 44
Dorr, John, 79
Eden, Brad, x
Fister, Barbara, 50
Friend, Linda, 88
Froehlich, Peter, 95
Gabler, Vanessa, x
Gilman, Isaac, x, 86
Gritten, Tim, 197
Grotophorst, Wally, 42
Harrison, Andrew, 223
Hawkins, Kevin S., x, xi, 170
Heller, Margaret, 68

Hess, M. Ryan, 26
Ho, Adrian K., xi, 144
Hoffman, Kristen, 102
Hoover, Jeanne, 30
Inefuku, Harrison W., x, 58
Jackson, Korey, x, xi
Johnston, Wayne, 132
Kahn, Meredith, xi
Kane, William, x, 210
Kanellopoulos, Lorena, 219
Kelly, Martin, 14
Khanna, Delphine, 116
Krefft, Jill, 36
Lally, Ann, 193
Lasou, Pierre, 120
Lawson, Anna, 237
Lee, Dan, 123
Lin, Yu-Hung, xi
Lindgren, Birgitta Hellmark, 225
Mangiafico, Paolo, 28
Marshall, Julie-Anne, 235
McCollough, Aaron, 138
McCready, Kate, xi, 158
McCulley, Lucretia, 181
McMillan, Gail, x, 207
Melton, Sarah, x, xi, 34
Mercer, Holly, 186
Mircea, Gabriela, 75
Mitchell, Catherine, x, 127
Morris, Jane, 2
Myers, Kim, 16
Nabe, Jonathan, 106
Neds-Fox, Joshua, x, 214
Newton, Mark, 20
Oberg, Johan, 70
Oleen, Jenny, 216
Oscarson, Mandy, 4
Ospina, Dana, 8
Owen, Brian, 104
Owen, Terry M., x, 147
Owen, Will, 164
Parkes, Nyssa, 227

Pavy, Jeanne, 162
Pekala, Shayna, 54
Pitcher, Kate, 109
Poley, Darren, 203
Polley, Ted, 56
Purple, Katherine, x
Ramsey, Ellen, 191
Rander, Jacklyn, 48
Reed, Marianne, 142
Reynolds, David, 62
Reznik-Zellen, Rebecca, 152
Riddle, Kelly, x, 183
Riley, Jenn, 73
Roach, Jonathan, 108
Robertson, Wendy, xi, 140
Rolfe, Alex, 40
Roosa, Mark S., 91
Royster, Paul, 160
Rouner, Andrew, xi
Rubin, Jeff, xi, 118
Ruddy, David, 22
Russell, John, 174
Russell, Judith C., 130

Scherer, David, x
Schlosser, Melanie, x, 81
Simser, Char, x, 64
Soper, Devin, 38
Spring, Kathleen, 66
Sprout, Bronwen, 125
Stenberg, Emily Symonds, 212
Stockham, Marcia, x, xi
Stone, Graham, 231
Swift, Allegra, x
Thomson, Mary Beth, xi
Tillinghast, Beth, 134
Tucker, Benjamin, 179
Walter, Scott, x, xi
Warren, Scott, 113
Watkinson, Charles, xi, 156
Wertzberger, Janelle, 46
Wesolek, Andrew, 12
Wills, Faedra, 189
Wolfe, Chip, 32
Wu, Somaly Kim, x, 166
Yates, Elizabeth, 6

INVITATION TO JOIN

The LPC promotes collaboration, knowledge sharing, and networking among library publishers and between libraries and other publishers by supporting an evolving, distributed range of publishing practices. We welcome membership applications from academic and research libraries from around the world.

ENGAGE WITH OUR INTERNATIONAL COMMUNITY OF PRACTICE:
- Connect with a diverse community of members. From small liberal arts colleges to large research universities, the LPC connects libraries with diverse profiles, interests, and areas of expertise.
- Access the members-only mailing list. Stay up to date with the latest from the LPC and the library publishing community.
- Benefit from special registration rates to LPC events. Attend our popular Library Publishing Forum at a discounted rate.

JUMP-START OR ENHANCE YOUR LIBRARY PUBLISHING INITIATIVES
- Access our shared documentation library. Consult resources created by your colleagues: everything from checklists for starting new journals to model MOUs.
- Participate in webinars with leading experts and vendors. Stay up to date with the latest in the theory and practice of library publishing with our regular webinar series.
- Browse our job board. Consult our archive of job descriptions for an up-to-date look at available jobs or to inform the development of new positions at your institution.

LEAD CHANGE IN SCHOLARLY COMMUNICATIONS AND PUBLISHING
- Gain voting rights in the Coalition. Ensure that your voice is heard in planning future directions and activities.
- Participate in national and international conversations. The LPC represents the interests of our community within a growing network of university presses, scholarly publishers, vendors, and professional associations.
- Serve on committees and task forces. Contribute directly to the advancement of the field by joining the dedicated group of volunteers who keep the LPC moving.

VISIT WWW.LIBRARYPUBLISHING.ORG FOR MORE INFORMATION.